TEACH YOURSELF BOOKS

# PUBLIC RELATIONS

Public Relations practice is the deliberate planned and sustained effort to establish and maintain mutual understanding between an organization and its public.

This book will help you to understand the basic principles underlying a vital subject and to teach yourself the rudiments of the techniques applied in dealing with Public Relations problems.

**Completely revised and updated edition**

## NOTE

Many changes are taking place in the organization of Public Relations in 1970. Readers are advised to check the up-to-date position with the appropriate bodies.

# TEACH YOURSELF BOOKS
# PUBLIC
# RELATIONS

## HERBERT LLOYD

*A Fellow and Past President of the Institute of Public Relations*
*A Member of the International Public Relations Association*
*A Member of Centre Européen des Relations Publique*

**TEACH YOURSELF BOOKS**

ST. PAUL'S HOUSE WARWICK LANE LONDON E.C.4.

First printed 1963
Second Edition 1970

Printed in Great Britain for
The English Universities Press Ltd., by
Cox and Wyman Ltd., London, Reading and Fakenham

# TO MY WIFE

*It has been said that there are three things a man should do before he dies: plant a tree, father a son, and write a book. This volume of the 'Teach Yourself' series is dedicated to the lady who made all three possible for me.*

# PREFACE

Public Relations practice is the deliberate planned and sustained effort to establish and maintain mutual understanding between an organization and its public.

This book will, it is hoped, help you to understand the basic principles underlying a vital subject and to teach yourself the rudiments of the techniques applied in dealing with Public Relations problems, the existence of which intelligent men and women are becoming increasingly aware.

It has been written to make you think and to take a fresh look at yourself—your organization, and your place in the community. For as Leonard L. Knott, a famous Canadian public relations practitioner, has pointed out, 'during the past half century business has spent millions on research, almost all of it devoted to the physical sciences and concerned with the development and production of new materials and machines. As a result, man can make silk almost as well and almost as cheaply as a worm can make it; he can manufacture cars with the power of two hundred horses and a speed faster than the wind—to travel on city streets where speeds greater than thirty miles an hour are impossible and on highways where speed and power cause death and destruction; he can send sound and pictures round the world in an instant, communicate with men on the moon and he can transport himself around the world faster than light so that he can leave one city today and arrive in another yesterday. All this research and all these marvels have not created Satisfied Man. The fruits of materialism are abundant but have a bitter taste because they cannot be used to conceal a failure to solve other more basic problems. The executive must now move from the physical to the social sciences. Turning his back on the atom, he needs to find out what people think and why; what they really want from life and why they react the way they do. Attitudes instead of products have become his scientific concern. Having conquered the physical world, business must at last begin to get acquainted with something that has been around longer than nylon or television or atomic power— the human mind and the spirit of man. Once he has done this, he can make use of the one important tool left to him, the power of Public Relations.'

Marshall McLuhan, Director of The Institute of Technology and Culture, Toronto, another great Canadian communicator, who said 'the medium is the message', has a theory that this is the first generation of the electronic age. He said they are different because the medium that controls their environment is not print—one thing at a time, one thing after another—as it has been for five hundred years. It is television, which is everything happening at once, instantaneously, and enveloping. Professor McLuhan in his book *Understanding Media* says that the new technologies of the electronic age, notably television, radio, the telephone and computers, make up a new environment; they are not merely *added* to some basic environment. He offers one startling prediction. Technologies to McLuhan, are all extensions of man. Clothes and houses extend his skin. The wheel extends his legs. Electricity extends his entire nervous system; a TV camera extends his eye and a microphone his ear. And now computers extend some of the activity that previously only went on inside man's brain. This is tantamount to an extension of consciousness. If you extend enough of it you have, in effect, pushed consciousness itself outside. Ours is a brand new world of 'allatonceness'. 'Time' has ceased, 'space' has vanished. We now live in a *global* village . . . a simultaneous happening . . .

# ACKNOWLEDGEMENTS

For permission to include copyright material the author is indebted to the authors and publishers of *Understanding Media: The Extensions of Man*, by Marshall McLuhan, Sphere Books Ltd., London; *Effective Public Relations* by Scott M. Cutlip and Allen H. Center, Prentice-Hall, Inc., New York; *Profitable Scriptwriting for TV and Radio*, by Gale Pedrick, C. Arthur Pearson, Ltd; *Practical Public Relations*, by Sam Black, Pitman; *Motivation Research*, by Harry Henry, Crosby Lockwood & Son, Ltd.; *The Dartnell Public Relations Handbook*, by Richard W. Darrow, Dan J. Forrestal, and Aubrey O. Cookman, The Dartnell Corporation; *Plain Talk about Public Relations*, by Leonard L. Knott, McClelland and Stewart Ltd., Canada; *The Nature of Public Relations*, by John Marston, McGraw-Hill Book Company; *Manual of Public Relations*, by Pat Bowman and Nigel Ellis, Heinemann; *How to Win the Business Battle* and *How to Get the Better of Business*, by Eric Webster, John Murray; *Planned Public Relations* by Frank Jefkins, Intertext Books; *Managing for Results*, by Peter F. Drucker, Heinemann; *International Public Relations Encyclopaedia*, by Peter Biddlecombe, Grant Helm; and especially to The Institute of Public Relations for references from *A Guide to the Practice of Public Relations*, Newman Neame, and for permission to reproduce data and recent Institute examination questions.

To Sir Thomas Lund, C.B.E., who inspired me.

Thanks are also due to James Derriman and to Philip Le Masurier for kindly reading the manuscript and making many valuable suggestions, and to R. Pinney, for his faith in me.

# CONTENTS

## Chapter One: How Public Relations Began

## Chapter Two: What is Modern Public Relations?

## Chapter Three: The Qualities Required

## Chapter Four: Research and Planning and Action

## Chapter Five: Press Relations

## Chapter Six: House Organs—Company Publications

## Chapter Seven: The Spoken Word—Speeches—Talks—Discussions

## Chapter Eight: Radio and Television

## Chapter Nine: Films

## Chapter Ten: Photographs

## Chapter Eleven: Exhibitions

## Chapter Twelve: Conferences

## Chapter Thirteen: Public Relations Ideas and Action

## Chapter Fourteen: The Institute of Public Relations and The Public Relations Consultants' Association

## Chapter Fifteen: Education for Public Relations in the Seventies

## Chapter Sixteen: Examination Questions and Diploma Syllabus

# 1  HOW PUBLIC RELATIONS BEGAN

There is no universally agreed history of Public Relations. Some people believe that throughout civilization there have been men and women who were skilled in the practice of Public Relations. Some will quote Queen Elizabeth I, others Wilberforce and the work which he did to secure the abolition of slavery. It may be that the craft Guilds of the Middle Ages had men who carried out functions which we, today, would term, in part, Public Relations, putting the case for the Guild, influencing public opinion and doing many other things which would, today, be regarded as being part of the normal work of a Public Relations practitioner.

Coming to more modern times, the first indication of the development of Public Relations as a separate activity came with the Industrial Revolution with its tremendous expansion of business and commerce, particularly in the United States. As the country prospered and its population increased rapidly, so the need for communication increased, particularly for manufacturers who wanted their wares to be known throughout the land. Here we see the beginnings of large scale advertising and publicity. The big firms employed men who were skilled in producing the kind of advertisements which were thought to be effective at the time. You may be interested in asking at your local library for copies of some old newspapers of seventy or eighty years ago. You will read some of the advertisements with astonishment and see how, although basically the same, the techniques of reaching the public have changed. However, it wasn't only the people who retailed goods who made use of publicity, but also some of the big industrialists in iron and steel and oil. They too employed men who could tell the public about their products. While those with goods to sell were engaging in ever-extending publicity campaigns, in the board rooms of the big organizations totally different types of problems were being encountered over publicity, particularly when a topic arose on which there was a conflict involving the public interest. For example, strikes and disasters were dealt with, to a very large extent by the policy at the time, which was that what the company decided to do was its own business and no concern at all of the community. It was every man for himself and genuinely a case of 'the public be damned'. This was the situation until the turn of the century when a gifted young American, with the unusual name of Ivy Ledbetter Lee, arrived on the scene.

Ivy Lee, the son of a Georgia minister and a graduate at Princeton University, started as a newspaper reporter, but after five years he left his underpaid job and eventually, in 1906, got his great chance. At that time the anthracite coal industry in America was going through a stage of severe strikes and Lee was given a free hand by its leaders to undertake the specialist service which he offered. This was to improve relations between the employers, the companies and the public, particularly the press, which had published bitter attacks on them, chiefly because of the violent methods they used to break strikes. Before taking on the job, however, he insisted, as he was always to do, on two things. The first was that he should deal with top management and the second was that he must be empowered to tell the whole of the facts, if he thought it wise to do so. The first of these conditions was quite revolutionary for, until that time, the men who had been handling publicity were very far removed from the top management of the great American industrial concerns and the second of his conditions, to be allowed to tell the public at large the truth about various matters that concerned the company, was indeed quite unique.

Lee, during this particular coal strike in 1906, issued a 'Declaration of Principles' which he sent to all the newspaper editors in the city. Lee's underlying principle was that the public could not be ignored in the usual manner of business up till then, nor fooled as they often had been by high-powered press agents. Lee conceived it his duty to inform them and this is what he wrote:

'This is not a secret press bureau. All our work is done in the open. We aim to supply news. This is not an advertising agency. If you think any of our matter ought properly to go to your business office, do not use it. Our matter is accurate, further details on any subject treated will be supplied promptly and any editor will be assisted, most cheerfully, in verifying any statement of fact. . . .

'In brief our plan is frankly and openly on behalf of business concerns and public institutions, to supply to the press and public of the United States prompt and accurate information concerning subjects which it is of interest and value to the public to know about.'

Now all this may seem very ordinary to you, reading it in the second part of the twentieth century, but at the time it was sensational. In one honest statement Ivy Lee had ripped aside the cloak of secrecy and callousness which had surrounded big business in its relations with the public until that time. Lee put his new idea to work throughout the coal strike and the journalists who were covering the event found that their work was made very much more simple, their reports were much more accurate and, indeed, even fuller because, whilst helping the reporters, Lee became the first to use the press handout system to a considerable extent.

B

The same year Ivy Lee was asked to help the Pennsylvania Railroad Company in connection with a serious accident which had occurred on its main line. Up until then when a disaster of this kind occurred, a veil of secrecy was drawn so that it was only with the utmost difficulty, if ever, that the public knew what had happened and how it had happened. To the consternation of the directors, Lee insisted on reversing the traditional procedure. He immediately made arrangements so that journalists could go to the scene of the accident and, in fact, special transport was provided to take them there. On their arrival they received every possible help, all their reasonable questions were answered, every facility given them and, to the astonishment of the Board, the Pennsylvania Railroad got the most favourable press it had ever had over an incident of this kind. Lee had demonstrated, triumphantly, that if you rightly and properly inform the public and take them into your confidence leaving them to form their own opinion from the true facts presented, then the public will always be prepared to understand and be fair.

In 1914 Lee became an adviser to John D. Rockefeller, Junior, the multi-millionaire. He advised him in connection with many of his gigantic business interests and always tried to make business a human affair. He was always studying the human element. He once said, 'I try to translate dollars and cents and stock and dividends into terms of humanity'. His father, John D. Rockefeller, Senior, at that time was not loved by the American public who hated his sternness and, particularly, his ruthlessness in connection with strike-breaking activities at the turn of the century. Ivy Lee realized that John D. Rockefeller at heart was a kindly old man and so, strange though it may seem, he persuaded him always to carry in his pocket a number of dimes to give to the children he met as he went about the streets. There are probably today, in America, a number of families who still treasure a ten-cent piece given to one of the members in his youth by the richest man in the United States and treasured as a symbol of good fortune.

Ivy Lee was the first man specifically to use the terms 'publicity' and 'advertising' in Public Relations work. In his footsteps there followed many other notable Americans.

In England the first man to practise Public Relations as we understand it today was Sir Stephen Tallents and I cannot do better than to tell you the story in his own words. They are reproduced from *A Guide to the Practice of Public Relations*, prepared by the Institute of Public Relations and published by Newman Neame. Sir Stephen called it 'By way of introduction . . .'

'In 1926 I was about to end a spell of work in Northern Ireland and my chief had come over from London to stay with us on a hill near Belfast. He discussed with me one evening what my next job should be. At the tail end of what seemed to me some rather forbidding suggestions, he mentioned casually and rather disparagingly that a grant of £1,000,000 a year was going begging in the shape of a sum for the benefit of the producers of the empire. This grant had been promised by Mr. Baldwin as compensation for his inability to fulfil a promise of preferences in favour of canned salmon and some other products. I pricked my ears at this clue, for the role of millionaire, however vicarious, appealed to me. So, in due course, I found myself as Secretary of a newly formed Empire Marketing Board, responsible for the planning and expenditure of an income of which two-thirds were allotted to the promotion of scientific agricultural research and the rest vaguely earmarked for publicity. Thus, in the spring of 1926 fairly well versed in the usual crafts of the Civil Servant, I leapt, all unequipped, into the dangerous world of publicity. I remember likening my lot to that of the baby (his own, happily rescued by an attendant) which a clergyman about that time, I was told, had thrown into a London swimming bath to prove his theory that every baby was a born swimmer.

'Inside the government service I found neither experience to guide nor encouragement to pursue this third of our programme, but from across the Atlantic came heartening tales of achievement, such as the saga of how Ivy Lee transformed not only the reputation, but also the personality of Rockefeller. I gratefully recall the enthusiasm of Mr. Amery, my Chairman and the generous expert help of William Crawford with his constant assurance that "No one knows anything about publicity", and of Frank Pick. Their support enabled me, if with no smooth passage, to rise to the surface. I have had a fellow feeling since for all young men and women facing up to a similar dive.

'My first publicity efforts started with the study of a report by the Imperial Economic Committee on Empire Fruits and was focused, if I remember rightly, on the task of selling Empire apples—a campaign which, I am happy to note, has been revived by producers home and overseas again, combining. I speak of "publicity" for the title "Public Relations" did not cross the Atlantic till seven years later when it caught the eye of Sir Kingsley Wood, puzzled to describe the role to which he had invited me at the Post Office, in a report of the American Telegraph and Telephone Company; but the publicity work of the Empire Marketing Board during the seven years of its existence grew to be akin to that of many a Public Relations Officer today.

'I tried to summarize my experience at the end of those seven years in a pamphlet called *The Projection of England*. Its contents make familiar enough reading today, but I well remember the pains that little work then cost me to produce. Now, looking back a quarter of a century on, I regard Public Relations work in its widest sense as one of the most far-reaching and important tasks of our time. I know it also, properly conducted, for a task not only requiring as much organizing ability as any straight-forward administration or business, but demanding also an element of flair and a capacity to understand and work with artists.'

This then was how Public Relations as we understand it today began.

The war of 1939–45 saw significant developments in the techniques of informing the public and much of the sound practice of today is based on good work done at that time at the Ministry of Information.

The post-war period has been one of rapid development. Government Departments, those engaged in commerce, industry, the professions—now use Public Relations with integrity and intelligence to establish and maintain mutual understanding between their organizations and the public.

Businesses large and small pay increasing attention to this important subject. Charitable organizations such as Oxfam publish their 'case histories' telling of the public relations campaigns by which they enlisted public support. There has been a tremendous advance in technology—transistors, tape recorders, television, now with colour; videotapes which enable you to see an immediate play-back of a TV programme, computers, 'instamatic' cameras, printing by using photography instead of type, photocopying and satellite communications have all brought about a revolution in the ways and means of informing the public.

# 2 WHAT IS MODERN PUBLIC RELATIONS?

The Institute of Public Relations defines Public Relations practice as the deliberate, planned and sustained effort to establish and maintain mutual understanding between an organization and its public. We shall look closely at each part of the definition in due course. First, let me give you some practical examples.

You have all seen the gas company doing some repairs to a main. There is the usual hole in the ground with a great pile of earth alongside, but sometimes, something else. A metal sheet on which is written 'The Blank Gas Board regrets any inconvenience which may be caused you in undertaking necessary repairs'.

Now, it is unlikely that the reading of that notice is going to encourage you to use more gas. You will only use the amount of gas that you require for cooking or heating. I doubt very much whether, as a result of reading that notice, you will at once purchase gas appliances. Then what is the object of the exercise? Who decided to put the notice there? Why? If you pause to think about this you will realize that it gives you rather a nice feeling to read such a notice. You say to yourself, the people at the gas board are human. They understand that holes in the ground and piles of earth, of which there seem to be so many nowadays, are a nuisance and that people don't like them, but they are usually necessary and so, when they have to open up the road, they try to do it in as nice a way as possible. As you ask yourself in a more searching way, you will find that it makes you think well of the organization and all connected with it. If the hole in the ground were not necessary and if it was not being done ultimately for the public good and advantage, but was being done by the neighbour next door who suddenly decided to dig a hole, we shouldn't feel very kindly towards him, even if he did put polite notices up, but the gas board are performing an inconvenient but necessary service well and they have done something to make us accept it with good grace and, consequently, they are quite in order in encouraging us to think well of them.

You may have seen a building site with hoardings all round to protect the public, but right in the middle is an opening marked 'Observation Platform'. To observe what? Well, you and I know that there is nothing more interesting or more enjoyable than watching other people working, particularly if they are digging an enormous hole in the ground with all kinds of the latest mechanical equipment. I suppose, in one way, it might be called a national pastime. So this huge firm, XYZ Limited, which undertakes building operations all over the world, has decided to put a small platform where passers-by can stand, safely, and look down at the workmen busy below. The chances of your ever instructing that particular firm to build a block of flats or an office skyscraper or a gigantic bridge are extremely remote. The chances that you will lease or even purchase the building on which they are now working when complete are unlikely. Then why have they done it? In rather the same way as the gas board, they know that building works usually mean noise and mess and dirt, lorries coming at all hours of the day and night taking away the earth and bringing materials, possibly to the annoyance of passers-by and of the neighbours. They know too of the curiosity we all have in wanting to see what's happening, particularly behind a hoarding at the back of which are all kinds of interesting noises. So they put up the observation platform and as you stand there watching the ant-like activity of those below, you probably feel, as I do, well disposed towards the firm. You say to yourself, well they do care about the public, they do treat us as human beings, they do try to understand us and, once again, probably quite unconsciously, a feeling of goodwill is built up in our minds towards this particular organization.

Now, this feeling will probably last for quite a time, when one sees their lorries on the road in future, long after the work we are looking at is completed, you will probably think again, unconsciously, 'Ah, a good firm, XYZ. That was an interesting building they put up at So and So, I remember how they built it.'

You may feel quite the same way when you see a certain type of advertisement in the paper. It doesn't really seem to sell anything, it may be a half page in *The Times* or some other national newspaper simply showing the picture of a magnificent building with the name of the firm underneath it. This is what is called Prestige Advertising, designed to keep before the public the image that the directors would like the public to have of the firm. Modern, successful and great. Also, here, in this half page, they are showing proof of their achievement. This is advertising used as a Public Relations medium. This shows, by the way, how closely Public Relations, Publicity and Advertising are connected. A little later on you will learn exactly what the differences between them are.

Looking at the two illustrations I have given, what both the gas board and the construction company did was a deliberate act on their part. There was nothing accidental about it. Someone in authority had decided, quite deliberately, to take definite action to show the public the kind of people they are. It was quite deliberate. It was planned. A workman didn't suddenly conceive the idea and get a sheet of hardboard and scrawl across it in chalk, 'Sorry for the mess, folks,' and neither did the construction company cover the entire construction with hoarding, leaving the public to peer through the entrance when open. No. In both cases it was not only deliberate, but it was planned as well and if you look closely at many of the other activities of these organizations you will almost certainly find that this wasn't a flash in the pan, this isn't the only thing that they do to try and make you feel good towards them. They do many other things as part of a Public Relations Plan. You will probably find, for example, that when they send out printed material it is attractive, it is easy to read, although I doubt very much whether any bill for gas can be attractive! Let us say you forgot to pay the bill. Have a look at the way in which a reminder sent to you is worded and you will probably find that the first one at any rate is polite and, although firm, courteous and quite an inducement to pay promptly. This wasn't always so and still isn't in the case of some organizations who swiftly send a very curt reminder written in red telling you of the dire consequences in seven or fourteen days unless you pay. You may argue that the latter way is probably more effective in making you settle your accounts promptly, but I doubt very much whether it would make you feel better disposed towards the organization which sends them out. You will also probably find that the construction company has some very good letters, pamphlets and brochures about their activities, which perhaps they make available to those being inconvenienced near the building site. They probably also produce special literature for schools and when, as they must do once a year, they send out a Chairman's report to all shareholders, you will probably find that it is very well done indeed. Clear, concise, telling the shareholders exactly what they want to know, keeping the Chairman's speech to a reasonable and readable length, putting in really interesting photographs about the expanding activities of the company and generally making the shareholders feel rather proud that they have got shares in it. It gives them a glow of

satisfaction to feel that this up to date, modern and prosper-
ous concern is something in which they have a stake. Now,
not all documents sent out by the boards of companies are
interesting to read. Some are very dull with long, uninteresting speeches full of platitudes and the only photograph in
the whole thing is an enormous one of the Chairman—
and who wants to look at him—except possibly his wife
and family ? No, this again is another example of the difference between a firm which has studied and practises Public
Relations and one that hasn't. After all, the report which
must be sent out by a company is a document, the contents
of which are laid down by the law and it must go to certain
people and as long as it contains precisely what the law
requires, then all is well, at least so far as the law is concerned. You may say, if a man has got shares in his company,
what does it matter what the annual report looks like as long
as it pays a good dividend. It isn't quite so simple as that.
You see, the firm may perhaps not do so well in one year
and you may feel that a firm which treats its shareholders
with very little consideration is really not an efficient firm
in the twentieth century, that it may not be able to hold its
own with growing competition from more modern companies and so you might decide to transfer your allegiance, to
sell your shares, and to take no real interest in the firm's
affairs. Nowadays you often read about 'take-overs'. One
company, looking at the balance sheet of another says to
itself that it could probably run it better and make more
money if it controlled its assets. So they decide to make a
'take-over bid' for the shares. Often the directors of the
other company don't want to be taken over at all. And they
will resist the attempt as strongly as possible. But who will
decide the fate of the company concerned ? Why, the shareholders. Now if they have been treated well in the past and
their sense of loyalty to the firm has been fostered, and this
means loyalty to and confidence in the directors too, then

they may refuse the offer for their shares and the take-over does not take place. So good public relations between a company and its shareholders can be very important indeed. But a good concern doesn't just regard you as a number in the Register of Shareholders, it thinks of you as an intelligent person and someone whom they hope will take an interest in their various activities. So, the annual report, in a certain way makes you feel well disposed towards them, but if the company were really no good at all and simply dressing up in attractive language, articles and brilliant photographs a record of dismal failure, then that would certainly not be Public Relations, it might even be a criminal offence.

The Chinese have an old proverb, 'You cannot carve rotten wood.' This is worth repeating. 'You cannot carve rotten wood.' What has this got to do with Public Relations? Just this, that sound Public Relations must have a worth-while product or idea or organization to put across to the public. It is true that many of the ways in which Public Relations is performed can be prostituted, in just the same way that any other specialist or professional skills can allegedly be practised by charlatans. This is fundamental and something that must be clearly understood. People who don't know a lot about Public Relations may say that it can be used to make people believe anything about anything. This just is not true and one of the most important first facts to be grasped if you are to understand the true nature of Public Relations is that it is founded on integrity.

Do you remember what the definition of public relations was? Public Relations practice is the deliberate, planned and sustained effort to establish and maintain mutual under-standing between an organization and its public. The public has a short memory and the pressure on it today, from all sides, the clamour made by people who are trying to attract attention, means that, to be sustained, the message must reach the public frequently. The various activities of Public Relations, such as the use of television, radio, posters, and letters which are sent to you asking you to do various things, are all linked together in a sustained campaign. Next, Public Relations is used to establish mutual understanding. Why 'mutual' ? This is another of the fundamental truths of Public Relations. Public Relations is a two-way affair. The whole time that an organization is taking active steps to try and influence you, so you in your turn are having a direct effect on the decisions being made by that organization. How is this possible ? You may not know any of the board or a single member of the staff. You may never have anything to do with them at all. How can it be said that you have anything to do with the mutual understanding between that company and the public ?

You are representative of all the people in this country, a member of the public, and a wise board always listens to the reactions and the opinions of the public. In recent years more and more people have answered a knock on their door to find a complete stranger standing there who is usually very polite and often quite interesting, who wants to ask you some questions about a product now being sold, about some campaign which is being conducted and, in the most courteous manner, asks whether you would mind giving some answers. The good-natured British public are usually quite prepared to do this. What is being done and why has that stranger called at your house ? Well, you are looking at another of the activities of Public Relations. I hasten to add that it is also a tool of advertising and a tool of salesmanship, for many of the things which are done in Public Relations are also done in the other two occupations I have mentioned. The stranger at your door is undertaking some market research and would like to ask you some questions. These questions are usually prepared very carefully indeed because if you have to look at hundreds of thousands of answers then you must be certain that your questions are put in a way which will elicit an unbiased answer and in which the results can be recorded and evaluated quickly and accurately. Market research, audience surveys and so on are designed and carried out because the organization wants to know what you are thinking and, even if you have never used the product, you cannot recollect ever having seen it advertised, you know nothing about it, your negative replies are of the utmost importance to the company concerned because they show, quite clearly, that some of their activities are in fact not being of any use at all. You are a perfectly intelligent person who goes about the town and yet has heard nothing at all about what they are doing! But, if you have got something to say, the Board will, in due course, spend much time looking at the reports from the firm which has done the research for them because, on your replies will depend, to a very great extent, the future activities of the company in certain ways. If the 'image' (which is the technical expression meaning the overall impression the company has upon you) if the image you have of the company or its product is a good one, they will know that they are on the right lines. If the image is a bad one, they will take steps to improve it.

You might like to look up the word 'image' in the Oxford English Dictionary. You will find some very curious meanings, but when we are talking about Public Relations the word 'image' really means 'the idea or conception'—in other words, if I say 'fast car' to you, immediately in your mind will come the image of a fast car. Ah, yes, but what kind of fast car? If you are fortunate enough to drive a particular sports car, you will immediately think of that make of car. If, on the other hand, you have never driven a car in your life but on one occasion were nearly knocked down by a 'Blank' car, then when I say 'fast car' you will, probably automatically, have the image of a 'Blank' car in your mind. When you hear a particular dance tune, depending upon the year in which it became popular, so you will respond. Certain groups of people of different ages will react in different ways, those who were courting at that time will, on hearing the tune, recollect very happy days spent, possibly, in carefree circumstances. These, then, are the 'images'. Images depend largely on the association of ideas, of which the more you know the more effective your Public Relations will be. There is a helpful book on psychology published in the *Teach Yourself* series. It is a very interesting subject and one with which Public Relations is closely concerned.

So, with many Public Relations activities, ideas and suggestions are brought to mind about a particular thing depending again upon what is done. The results of your thinking when known and if appropriate, are incorporated into the overall Public Relations Plan of the questioning firm.

All good plans have objectives. Sometimes short-term ones and long-term ones. Public Relations plans are made with objectives constantly in mind. They are usually the result of accurate research and much thought.

Consider now the organization with whom you are associated. What do people think about it? Do you really know? If not, some skilled research is called for. What would you like people to think about it? Would that reputation be deserved? If not, put your own house in order first. Improve the product, the service or whatever it is you give the public. Doing this may entail a quite separate internal Public Relations programme dealing with staff.

If you have a fine product—give an excellent service—people will do business with you *provided they know about you*. A business must be efficient to survive, but nowadays it must also be seen to be efficient. Not just to customers, employees, and shareholders, but to the man in the street. Every business is part of the community and you and your firm are becoming more and more interdependent with those around you. Public Relations is not something that you can make up your mind to have or not as you please. Public Relations is something you have, whether you want it or not. It is part of the job of managing a business, and should be done with just as much expertise as is applied to any other management functions such as finance, production or marketing.

There are a number of other words you will come across which seem to be important in studying this subject. Let us have a look at some of them.

Peter Biddlecombe in his *International Public Relations Encyclopedia* published by Grant Helm gives the following definitions:

*Public Relations:* There have been many attempts to define public relations. Here is a selection of the more appropriate:

The Institute of Public Relations: 'Public Relations is the deliberate, planned and sustained effort to establish and maintain mutual understanding between an organization and its publics.'

Edward L. Bernays: 'Public Relations is the attempt by information persuasion and adjustment to engineer public support for an activity cause, movement or institution.'

John W. Hill: 'The management function which gives the same organized and careful attention to the asset of goodwill as is given to any other major asset of business.'

Herbert M. Baus: 'Public Relations is a combination of philosophy, sociology, economics, language, psychology, journalism, communication and other knowledges into a system of human understanding.'

Charles Plackard: 'Merely human decency which flows from a good heart.'

Fortune Magazine: 'Good performance, publicly appreciated because adequately communicated.'

Robert Heilbroner: 'Public Relations is Dale Carnegie—winning friends and influencing people—writ large.'

George F. Meredith, former president of the American Public Relations Association: 'Everything involved in achieving a favourable opinion.'

The International Public Relations Association, The Hague, May 1960: 'Public Relations is a management function, of a continuing and planned character, through which public and private organizations and institutions seek to win and retain the understanding sympathy and support of those with whom they are or may be concerned—by evaluating public opinion about themselves, in order to correlate, as far as possible, their own policies and procedures, to achieve by planned and widespread information more productive cooperation and more efficient fulfilment of their common interests.'

Carl Byoir, one of the most successful U.S. publicists: 'Public Relations is whatever the individual practitioner thinks it is.'

Scot M. Cutlip and Allen H. Center, authors of *Effective Public Relations*, Prentice-Hall Inc.: 'The communication and interpretation and the communications and ideas from an institution to its publics and the communication of information, ideas and opinions from those publics to the institution, in a sincere effort to establish a mutuality of interest and this achieves the harmonious adjustment of an institution to its community.'

Max K. Adler, one of the most experienced and best known of market researchers: 'Its object is not to sell a product, but to produce a favourable image of a company and improve on it, if necessary.'

Frank Jefkins in his book *Public Relations in World Marketing*: 'P.R. means what it says—relations with the public. It is practically a self defining term. It aims to create and maintain confidence. It is a system of communications to create goodwill. It produces that intangible quality or asset—goodwill—and earns credit for achievements.'

The definition of public relations was taken a step further on October 23rd, 1964, when for the first time it was officially defined and recognized by the French Government. The official text was issued by the Ministry of Information. And on November 1st, 1964, it appeared in the Journal Officiel de la Republic Francaise, the official gazette of the French Government. It was the first time any government had officially defined P.R. The decree was as follows:

'The duties of a public relations practitioner whether he belongs to the staff of a firm or is an independent consultant, are to devise and submit to the firms or organizations employing his services the means of establishing and maintaining good relations, based on mutual confidence, with the public and keeping it informed of their achievements and, more generally, of all matters relating to their operations. These duties may also be extended to include the relations of firms with their own staff. The public relations practitioner is responsible for implementing the recommended policy and for measuring results.

'The information he supplies about the organization must in all cases carry mention of its source, be strictly objective and be absolutely free of propaganda, commercial publicity or advertising content. The Press Officer carries out the duties defined above as a specialist in relations with the following information media: press, films, radio and television. The duties of a public relations practitioner and of a press officer are incompatible with their practising at the same time as a professional journalist or advertising agent. The only remuneration for public

C

relations or press work shall be the fees of the client or salary of the employer on whose account this work is undertaken.'

This translation by Claude Chapeau appeared in 'Eleven Years of Public Relations', a brochure prepared by Galeries Orleanzises, France, and published in April 1965.

In 1969 the British definition was accepted by a Select Committee of the House of Commons set up to consider the Declaration of Members' Interests, when a deputation of the Institute of Public Relations headed by the author of *Teach Yourself Public Relations* gave evidence before it.

Lucien Matrat, public relations manager of Union Industrielle des Petroles-UIP and Council Member of the International Public Relations Association: 'Public Relations is a mode of behaviour and a manner of conveying information with the object of establishing and maintaining mutual confidence, based on mutual knowledge and understanding, between an organization—a corporate body carrying out various functions or activities —and the different sections of the public, internal and external, that are affected by some or all of these functions or activities.'

*Publicity:* It is the function of publicity to tell the story. The conventional dictionary definition is, however, being in the state of being widely known. Basically, publicity is information which an editor will print because he believes it will interest his readers. Every item carried by the press, radio and television can be described as publicity for someone or something. Possibly the best definition is offered by Cutlip and Center: 'The dissemination of information, making matters public from the point of view of one who wishes to inform others. Systematic distribution of information about an institution or an individual.'

The International Public Relations Association adopted the following definition at The Hague in May 1960: 'The use of the word "Publicity" should be confined to describing an effect on public opinion resulting from activity or inactivity in the fields of public relations, advertising or propaganda.'

*Press Agentry:* Cutlip and Center say that this is the creation of publicity-worthy events and the use of brass bands and barkers, if necessary, to attract attention to some person or something.

Biddlecome: 'A press agent is engaged to get press coverage and press clippings. He pulls stunts and stages events. He gives journalists tipoffs and places stories with particular newspapers. There are four main types of press agent: the film press agent, employed by the film studios; the radio and television agent, who is employed by the networks; the theatrical press agent, who is employed either by the stage company or the management of the theatre, and the personal press agent, who works for individual people, either film stars, actors, writers or people both in and trying to be in the public eye.

*Press Relations:* Press Relations is that function of Public Relations which aims at earning and retaining confidence—on the part of those conducting and working in the many and various media of broadcasting, newsreels, radio and television—in the treatment of its own news by an organization or institution, not least through an efficient information service using all appropriate means.

*Propaganda:* The most notorious definitions were offered by Goebbels: 'an instrument of politics, a power for social control' . . . 'The function of propaganda is not essentially to convert; rather its function is to attract followers and to keep them in line' . . . 'The task o propaganda, given suitable avenues, is to blanket every area of human activity so that the environment of the individual is changed to absorb the (Nazi) movement's world view.'

Originally it meant simply spreading a belief, but its misuse, particularly during the last fifty years, has brought it into disrepute. So that today people regard propaganda as untrue or one-sided statements.

*Advertising:* The International Public Relations Association adopted the following definition at their meeting at The Hague in May 1960: 'The use of communications channels paid for by an organization or institution in order to present what it wants to say, in the way it chooses, and to audiences of its own selection—so as to give information and promote sales, either directly or indirectly.' The Advertising Association offers a more simple version: 'Advertising is the means of making known in order to sell goods or services.'

*Promotion:* The commercial manipulation of information, persuasion and influence. A publicity campaign for a product, person or organization.

*Marketing:* On September 8th, 1966, the Council of the Institute of Marketing defined marketing as: 'The management function which organizes and directs all those business activities involved in assessing and converting customer purchasing power into effective demand for a specific product or service and in moving the product or service to the final consumer or user so as to achieve the profit target or other objectives set by a company.' This was based, to a large degree, on a definition offered by Leslie Rodger in his book, *Marketing in a Competitive Economy* (1965), Hutchinson: 'Marketing is the primary function which organizes and directs the aggregate of business activities involved in converting consumer purchasing power into effective demand for a specific product or service and in moving the product or service to the final consumer or user so as to achieve the company-set profit or other objectives.' This superseded the previous Institute definition, which had been in use for about five years: 'Marketing is the creative management function which promotes trade and employment by assessing consumer needs and initiating research development to meet them. It coordinates the resources of production and distribution of goods and services; determines and directs the nature and scale of the total effort required to sell profitably by the maximum production to the ultimate user.'

The main difference between the old and the new definitions are the deletion of the word 'creative'; the closer identification of marketing techniques with business and marketing objectives with company objectives.

The P.R. practitioner has a number of roles to play in a marketing operation. He is responsible for overall consumer relations and the establishment of a favourable climate of opinion towards the product. He takes part in product planning and reports public attitudes by testing the role of the product. And the practitioner also decides the method and timing of the introduction to the public. Advertising, promotion, activities of the sales force, must all be integrated into a comprehensive programme in order to achieve the maximum impact and effectiveness.

*Sales Promotion:* Marketing activities, apart from personal selling, advertising and publicity, which stimulate demand from both the trade and the consumer. The American Marketing Association suggests such things as displays, shows and expositions, demonstrations 'and various non-recurrent selling efforts not in the ordinary routine'. It differs from advertising in three important respects. Advertising is handled by media owners. Sales promotion is handled directly by the company itself. Advertising deals, necessarily, in more general terms than sales promotion. Companies could not exist without advertising but they could exist without sales promotion, which is only a bridge between advertising and direct selling.

You will notice that the words 'publics' is used—not 'the public'.

The public consists of innumerable groups with common interests. Men, women, teenagers, children, retired people, teachers, housewives, ex-servicemen, householders, car owners, the list is literally endless. In considering any public relations problem the identification of the sectors of the public or 'the publics' concerned is of the utmost importance. The plan evolved may deal in quite different ways with teenagers and retired people.

Some say that Public Relations is 'doing good and getting the credit for it'. To get the credit you must deserve it. So often Public Relations begins at home. Once your house is in order you can open the front door and put your plans into action.

Finally, in his excellent book *Practical Public Relations*, published by Pitman in 1966, Sam Black, O.B.E., F.R.S.A., F.I.P.R., summarizes as follows:

Public Relations practice includes:
1. Everything that is calculated to improve mutual understanding between an organization and all with whom it comes into contact, both within and outside the organization.
2. Advice on the presentation of the 'public image' of an organization.
3. Action to discover and eliminate sources of misunderstanding.
4. Action to broaden the sphere of influence of an organization by appropriate publicity, advertising, exhibitions, films, etc.
5. Everything directed towards improving communications between people or organizations.

Public Relations is *not*:
1. It is not a barrier between the truth and the public.

2. It is not propaganda to impose a point of view regardless of the truth, ethics and the public good.

3. It is not publicity aimed directly at achieving sales, although public relations activities can be very helpful to sales and marketing efforts.

4. It is not composed of stunts or gimmicks. These may be useful at times to put over ideas, but fail completely if used often.

5. It is not unpaid advertising.

6. It is not merely Press relations, although Press work is a very important part of most public relations programmes.

7. Public relations in central and local government is non-political. It is to promote democracy and not to advance the policy of any political party.

# 3 THE QUALITIES REQUIRED

A lot of people think to themselves that they are quite sure they could make a great success of a career in Public Relations. When you ask them why they often reply that they just like meeting people. But just to like meeting people is not enough. If you are really to succeed in Public Relations and you are quite serious about it then you will have to be prepared to work hard, to study hard and to make the very best of your natural talents.

You often hear the expression that so and so has a 'flair' for this or a 'flair' for that, but if you look at the facts closely you will often find that this reputation of a 'flair' is built up on one or two lucky incidents and that the success has come apparently without effort or it is the result of hard study and hard work. It may well be that a few of you who read this book are what might be called 'born' Public Relations men and women. But probably very few. On the other hand it is probable that very many of you who read this book, if you take a little time and trouble will, in fact, become reasonably competent in understanding and practising Public Relations in whatever sphere you choose.

It is true that to do Public Relations well you have to like people but it is much more than that, you have to want to serve them. You have to want to help them, to take many of their problems off their shoulders and provide a satisfactory solution. It is this sense of service which, to a large extent, distinguishes the practice of Public Relations from publicity or propaganda or advertising or salesmanship. What then are the qualities that are required? Do you need to have a university degree or a grammar school education ? Not necessarily. But to take the Institute of Public Relations Certificate Course you must have a minimum educational qualification of four 'O' level subjects in the General Certificate of Education, one of which must be English language or literature, or you must have passed another examination acceptable to the I.P.R. Council as being of an equivalent standard. Whatever your educational background if you are prepared to study, then there is no reason why you should not understand Public Relations. Of course, you must be reasonably intelligent, but other qualities form a rather strange list. Without preaching a sermon, you must have the good old-fashioned virtues. You must have honesty and integrity and character. These are essential. A sense of curiosity about words, people, things, places, in fact the wider your general knowledge the better your Public Relations will be. It is often quite astonishing how knowledge gained in one sphere can quite unexpectedly help you to solve a problem in another. The ability to persuade people reasonably and nicely and pleasantly is a great help. We have all met the man who tries to hammer his point of view down our throats and we generally end up by disliking him and with a strong conviction, often proved right, that his ideas must be weak if he has to try and prove them so violently. On the other hand we all have friends whose views we respect and whose opinions we listen to with confidence, because not only are they usually sound but they are put in a reasonable way. This is an invaluable quality in Public Relations. It's a help if people like you and there is no need to be modest about this. Being cheerful is an asset. After all, there are so many dismal people in this world that to find some who are cheerful (without overdoing it— especially first thing in the morning!), makes you feel well disposed towards them and one can generally assume that their own personal Public Relations are in a satisfactory state. Of course, we can all be disconcerted with the over-vigorous, 'Hail, fellow, well met!' hearty slap-on-the-back type of greeting. We are not talking about forced cheerful-ness, but just a kind of happy certainty that some people have about them; they seem to be enjoying life and making the most of it. They're confident, they feel they are putting something into life and, consequently, they are taking more out. Talking about taking—resist if you can the temptation and try not to take yourself too seriously. One of the most interesting Public Relations men I ever met made a pact with a number of his close friends whereby he gave each of them a pin and made them solemnly promise that if ever he became pompous, conceited or bumptious they would quietly come up and stick it in him. You may find attempting to do Public Relations a few who give you the impression that they are following some strange and curious craft whose innermost secrets have to be carefully guarded and who talk in a kind of mumbo-jumbo that only the initiated can understand after years of training! They are not succeeding in doing sound Public Relations. You should have a flair for words. Your reading should be wide—every type of reading, from *The Times* to cartoon strips, from the Bible to the most modern short story writer. It is only in this way that you will acquire a command of words and the ability to handle them with confidence. Here again, too, there is a wide range of books published in the *Teach Yourself* series which you will find useful and which are listed at the end of this chapter. The good Public Relations man is sensitive. He is al-ways sensitive, not in the sense of being ready to take offence lightly, but sensitive to atmosphere, to other people's feelings, to situations, to appreciating what is happening and to what is likely to happen. This sensitivity, or one might almost call it a sixth sense, is something which most people acquire as they grow older and one should do every-thing possible to cultivate it. There are so many other things which can help you, and some of the following are probably the most useful qualities you can have.

A knowledge of how the country is governed, how laws are made or by-laws adopted by your local authority. How justice is administered in your local magistrates court, in the county court and in the High Court. How newspapers are made. What journalists and editors do. Some knowledge of psychology—what makes people tick and why do people react in certain ways. An appreciation of art, colour, form, type and print. Business experience, buying, selling, commerce and banking. Some knowledge of films and how they are made. An interest in television and radio. Some of these topics are dealt with in greater detail later on in the book, but it really is quite surprising the amount of knowledge that you can pick up by intelligent reading, by talking to men who are in jobs connected with the topics mentioned, by going to see them at their work where facility visits are made available and generally broadening and widening your experience in this way.

Having a good imagination helps. Can you visualize what the implications are of a given situation and see what the result is likely to be? Let me give you an example. You meet a stranger in a friend's house and it turns out that he is about to build a factory which will employ several hundred people on the outskirts of a town which, up until then, had been almost exclusively agricultural. A typical sleepy country town. Maybe the people in that town will probably be very pleased, but wait a moment, what people? Possibly some of the shopkeepers, the inn keepers, the café proprietors and the garage owners, but there will probably be quite a number of people around that town who will be opposed to the idea. They will resent a lot of strangers coming from the city and spoiling their sleepy market town. Then there may be people living there who had deliberately chosen that town to which to retire. Maybe

they had returned to spend their last days in peace and
quiet where they had spent their childhood and the last
thing in the world they want is to have their peace disturbed.
Others may be frightened that the staff they now employ at
moderate wages will be enticed away to work in the new
factory. Farmers, with good land on the edge of the town,
may not relish the idea of it being taken away from them
and used for industrial development. The more artistic
among the community may say that the whole look of the
town will be spoilt. It will become ugly. It will become
industrialized. Others may say the schools will become overcrowded. While you are listening to news of the project,
you may begin to visualize some of the problems which he
will almost certainly have to face as his factory development
takes place. A good Public Relations man hearing the story
of the siting of the new factory would quickly analyse the
basic problems which will have to be met. He would visualize situations which could arise and having so to speak
looked into the future, would then sit down and with the
utmost care and skill devise a plan with an objective and a
list of the means by which programmes based on it would
be put into operation. In the example above the ultimate
objective would be to have, on the outskirts of that sleepy,
market town, a highly efficient, successful and happy factory
completely integrated into the communal life of the town
so that everyone benefited; the factory workers from the
knowledge that they can spend their leisure hours in pleasant surroundings among people whom they like and by
whom they are liked, so that they feel they belong; and the
town people accepting graciously that the newcomers are
not hostile and that the fresh faces and fresh ideas will not
mar in any way their amenities, tradition and way of life.
Do you see now how imagination helps?

To sum up, one needs honesty, integrity, character,
intelligence, imagination, ability to write, to speak in public,

administrative capacity, a wide general knowledge and a very high ethical standard. Sympathy, understanding, leadership, sound judgement, ideas and courage. Incidentally some of the best Public Relations practitioners are women. It offers them a splendid career. This may sound rather like a religious cult, or some esoteric philosophy, but do not be disheartened. What is important is that you do have the very clear idea, right from the start, that Public Relations has, in fact, a high standard of ethics. Did you know that Public Relations practitioners throughout the world had agreed on a Code of Conduct? The Institute of Public Relations has a Code which has much in common with that of the International Public Relations Association agreed in Venice in May 1961. The Institute's Code has recently been revised. The new draft Code, which is subject to approval at the annual general meeting of the I.P.R. in November 1970, is as follows:

### I.P.R. Code of Conduct

1. A member, in the conduct of his professional activities, shall respect the public interest and the dignity of the individual. It is his personal responsibility at all times to deal fairly and honestly with his client or employer, past or present, with his fellow members and with the public.

2. A member shall not knowingly disseminate false or misleading information, and shall use proper care to avoid doing so inadvertently. He has a positive duty to maintain integrity and accuracy.

3. A member shall not engage in any practice which tends to corrupt the integrity of the media of communication.

4. A member shall not create, use or act for any organization apparently serving an announced cause but in fact promoting an undisclosed interest of the member, his clients or his employer. It is his duty to ensure that the

actual interest of any such organization with which he may be concerned is adequately declared.

5. A member shall not disclose (except upon the order of a court of competent jurisdiction) or make use of information given or obtained in confidence from his employer or client, past or present, for personal gain or otherwise, without express consent.

6. A member shall not represent conflicting or competing interests without the express consent of the parties concerned after full disclosure of the facts.

7. A member, in the course of his professional services to his employer or client, shall not accept payment either in cash or kind for those services from any other source without the express consent of his employer or client.

8. A member shall not negotiate or agree terms with a prospective employer or client on the basis of payment contingent upon specific future results.

9. A member seeking employment or new business by direct and individual approach to a potential employer or client shall take all reasonable steps to ascertain whether that employment or business is already carried out by another member. If so, it shall be his duty to advise the other member in advance of any approach he proposes to make to the employer or client concerned. (Nothing in this clause shall be taken as inhibiting a member from the general advertisement of his services.)

(Two clauses, 10 and 11, have been drafted to deal with the employment of Members of Parliament, and one of these would require any such employment by Institute members to be entered on a register kept by the General Secretary. These clauses have still to be discussed by the Institute's Council.)

12. A member shall not knowingly injure the professional reputation or practice of another member, but if such a member has reason to believe that another member

has been engaged in practices which may be in breach of this Code, it shall be his duty to inform the Institute.

13. A member who knowingly causes or permits another person or organization to act in a manner inconsistent with this Code shall himself be deemed to be in breach of it.

14. Conduct of any kind detrimental to the interests of the Institute or the profession of public relations shall be deemed to be a breach of this Code.

15. A member shall uphold this Code, shall cooperate with fellow members so doing and in enforcing decisions on any matter arising from its application. It is the duty of all members to assist the Institute in implementing this Code, and the Institute will support any member so doing. Anyone who wishes to have the definitive text of the I.P.R. Code should write to the General Secretary, who will be happy to supply a copy.

You may not have realized that Public Relations practice had a code and it has been introduced quite deliberately at an early stage in the book because it will help if what you read subsequently is read with the Code in mind. In America there is a slightly different Code as indeed there is in Australia and Canada, but basically all are the same and so, if after reading this chapter you feel that Public Relations is for you then it probably is and you can begin to consider the various ways in which Public Relations work is done. It is done by means which are called Media. In this case it means the agency or the means by which something is accomplished.

You will find at the end of this book a list of reference works which will be extremely useful to you in your Public Relations work. Some are absolutely essential, but you will find it well worth while early in your studies to provide yourself with a really good dictionary and get into the habit, if you come across a word the meaning of which you are not quite certain, of looking it up there and then. It is usually only in this way that you will remember what the word means in future.

Quite apart from the list of references, the *Teach Yourself* series contains the following volumes which you will find invaluable in giving you a grounding in subjects of use in Public Relations practice. They are:

| | |
|---|---|
| Advertising | Business organisation |
| Economics | Salesmanship |
| The Law | Psychology |
| Express Yourself | Public Speaking. |

# 4 RESEARCH AND PLANNING AND ACTION

The three stages in the planning and bringing into action of a Public Relations Plan are:

1. Research
2. Plan
3. Action

All sound planning is based on solid facts, and the facts have to be found out about any organization whatever its nature—from the one-man business to the commercial giant. Public Relations like charity begins at home and you cannot start effective public relations until you have put your own house in order. To do this it may and probably will entail a quite separate Public Relations programme to deal with internal relations—covering staff—trade unions—and all the other major factors involved in first-class management.

It was once said 'There are no such things as statistics—There are only people—and the things that affect people.' All Public Relations activities depend for their success on people—people on the staff—the heads of departments—the board of directors and above all the head of the firm. It is essential to enlist his full support. Public Relations is today a function of top management. No programme can succeed without its support. Your Public Relations programme can be ambitious and cover the whole of a large company's activities for the next ten years or it can be quite modest, dealing with only one aspect of a one man firm. The more time you spend on careful planning the more successful your programme is likely to be.

D

These are the questions to which you must produce clear written answers:

1. What is the object of the plan?
2. What precise problems are you trying to solve?
3. To what extent will that object be furthered by Public Relations?
4. Who is going to carry out the programme?
5. How is the plan to be administered?
6. What media will you use?
7. How much will it cost?

In the example already quoted of the company which was to build a new factory on the outskirts of the sleepy market town, the answers might read briefly as follows:

1. The object is to establish a new factory successfully and harmoniously.
2. The main problem to be solved is the happy integration of the newcomers with the residents.
3. The objective will be furthered almost entirely by Public Relations.
4. The plan will be administered by the Board of Directors.
5. The programme will be carried out by Tom Smith with supporting staff.
6. The media used for own staff, local residents and all publics concerned will include:

Speeches
Talks
Discussions
Films
Film Strips
Printed material of all kinds including:

Direct Mail Letters
Posters
Press announcements
Press advertisements
House Publications

Radio—possible—for local news programmes
Television        „   „   „   „
Exhibitions—model of new factory on display
Special events—visits of senior forms of appropriate
                local schools to see modern building
                construction.

7. The costs will depend on the amount the Board are prepared to allocate for a programme of this kind. It should be possible in an efficient firm to cost this fairly accurately beforehand. But remember—Good Public Relations cost money.

The foregoing is a rough outline of the sort of thinking which is essential before work starts seriously on the plan.

The first thing to put in hand is research. Most people fall into the trap of thinking they know how they stand in other people's esteem—how popular the firm is with customers—and so forth. Very often the truth is quite different from what they fondly imagine. No good Public Relations can be done without sound research. Unless you know the facts—and they must be *facts* not just off-the-cuff opinions —you cannot accurately diagnose the Public Relations problems to be solved.

It may well be that what other people think of you is more important than what you think of yourself. Ignorance of the views of others can hurt you.

Research, planning and action are parts of a continuous, never ceasing operation, and what people think about the company plays a vitally important part in planning.

If for example the Company was going to build the new factory in an industrial area with a high rate of unemployment and with the utmost co-operation of both central and local government then obviously the problems to be solved would be quite different—because of what people think about it. In this case the main Public Relations problem might be to induce key staff to move with their wives and families into less congenial surroundings.

## 1. Research

You cannot do too much research, for only in this way can true Public Relations be done on a two-way basis. You must listen more than you talk, and find out what people really know and believe. Try and anticipate trouble, for the art of administration is the art of anticipation. Once you have your information you should see that sound reports receive the attention and support they deserve from top management.

You should endeavour to keep as simple as possible the fundamental aim of the research. It is easy to be too ambitious and then find that your results are ineffective. The usual way in which research is done is as follows:

First—Gather together all the available data, facts, reports, histories, previous plans, minutes and resolutions that are relevant. Remember that in business you will probably need to compile a separate file of data dealing with competitors.

Next—List the groups of the public affected. They may be all the people living in a town or the 'influence formers' such as teachers, doctors, solicitors and bank managers. Then find out what their attitudes are—always bearing in mind the objectives. Analyse the results and assess the reasons for the opinions held. Apply the results in diag-

nosing the problems to be solved, and base the programme on the solution of these problems.

The country is composed of groups of people who exercise a power much greater than their numbers. People like
politicians, solicitors, doctors, accountants, teachers, bankers, and so on. These have been carefully analysed by
Anthony Sampson in his remarkable book *The Anatomy of
Britain Today*, Hodder and Stoughton, 1967. Just as the
country is divided into these sections, so is any city or town.
Look at the area in which you live and you will find that it is
really a comparatively small group of men and women who
run things; the local council, societies, charities, sports and
so forth. So if you are going to list the people who matter,
Anthony Sampson's book is an invaluable guide to the way
to do it.

You cannot get accurate information by merely reading
the local newspaper and chatting to a few of the oldest
inhabitants.

Research today is a highly skilled operation but it need
not be expensive. Often a 'pilot scheme' in which the views
of small representative sections of the public are canvassed
will provide you with sufficient information upon which to
base simple and effective Public Relations programmes.

For more ambitious schemes experts must be called in.
The framing of questions for opinion research is in itself a
highly complex psychological study. If you get the opportunity, see a film which is available from Worldwide Films
on 16 mm. called 'The Pollsters' and you will appreciate
this immediately.

Harry Henry in his classic *Motivation Research*, published by Crosby Lockwood & Sons, Ltd., says 'While it is
true that there still exist a number of short-sighted manufacturers who will cheerfully authorize a manufacturing
and promotional budget of half a million pounds or so, and

yet develop an excruciating cramp in the pocket book at the suggestion that two or three thousand should first be spent in checking that the whole effort is being made in the right direction, the majority of successful manufacturers now accept the fact—with resignation if not with joy—that between 2 per cent and 3 per cent of any promotional budget *must* be spent in what military language calls "intelligence" . . . and what is vital in the study of a market is to know not only *what* the pattern is but also *why*. . . .'

And now a word about opinion polls.

Opinion polls are not always right—but they are seldom hopelessly wrong. A sound answer can usually be obtained if the poll is carefully planned and organized. It is often extremely useful if facts have to be ascertained quickly. The carrying out of an opinion poll is a job for an expert—either to undertake the whole operation or at least to advise on the field to be covered, the size of the poll, the exact wording of the questions and the method by which answers are to be secured and results analysed, collated and presented. Few organizations have all the information they require and you would do well to include at least one specific research project in your Public Relations plans for each year. But the success of a poll ultimately depends upon the response it gets. As a first step towards 'putting your own house in order' internal polls of the staff in your employ can produce most useful results which can form the basis of a staff Public Relations programme. Questions about working conditions, security, opportunities for promotion, practice, amenities and so on can be not only disconcertingly revealing but salutary to management. If you have a high percentage staff 'turnover' you probably need a good survey quickly.

Care should be taken over the timing of a survey. If you put one in hand immediately after an all round wage increase you may not get a true picture of the attitude of employees to employers generally. They should also be so organized that those who are called upon to provide answers have adequate time and facilities to do so. If you do carry out a successful staff survey you should expect a number of benefits. The morale of the entire staff should be raised—and weaknesses revealed. The organization's efficiency will have been critically examined—adverse and constructive criticism being received. You will know the extent to which your staff are informed of the things they ought to know. The whole system of communication should become better and misunderstandings cleared up.

Experience has shown that surveys, far from upsetting employees, if well done, have quite the opposite effect. But if you have trade union officials and members in your organization then obviously whatever is put in hand should be done with their fullest support and co-operation. You must consider carefully and with integrity the extent to which the findings of the survey are to be made available to the staff and to the public and the action to be taken on the findings.

If action is taken you should tell the staff that it is being done as a direct result of the survey.

It's no use putting a survey in hand just for the sake of having a survey. It must be done for a specific purpose in furtherance of a clearly defined Public Relations objective. You may realize there is a problem—yet have no precise information as to its true nature or extent. It may touch retirement, pensions, training schemes, publications, salaries, wages, conditions of work, and service—or any of the hundred and one facets of modern commercial and industrial organization.

The Dartnell Corporation of London and Chicago have a standard employee opinion poll available to companies and consultants for use in analysing the attitudes of employees. It can be self administered by the company or consultant making the survey, although it is recommended that the valuation be done by an outside firm.

Dr. Mark Abrams, one of the foremost exponents of surveys in Great Britain wrote a splendid little book some years ago entitled *Social Surveys in Action* (Heinemann), which gives a sound basic knowledge of polls and surveys and their techniques.

Here again advice can always be obtained from the Institute of Public Relations.

Dealing with the general opinion poll, the survey should be made objective and the following suggestions may be helpful:

1. Start off with a 'know-nothing attitude'.
2. Conduct survey to learn—not prove.
3. Avoid preconceived ideas of results.
4. Strive for absolute accuracy.
5. Apply stiff accuracy tests to both desirable and undesirable results.
6. Don't hide unpleasant results—tell the whole truth.
7. Use a scientifically accurate sample.
8. Include questions to check against known facts.
9. Avoid complicated unexplainable methods.
10. Explain method fully in all published reports.
11. Point out any weaknesses or limitations in your method.
12. State sources clearly for all outside information used.
13. Don't extend results unless you definitely state the size of your sample.

*(Dartnell Public Relations Handbook 1967)*

Whether you do a survey yourself or bring in an expert the above 'check list' will be useful in satisfying yourself and the top management of your organization that you are on the right lines.

Incidentally is the incoming mail at your firm ever analysed with Public Relations in mind? Are complaints as well as praise carefully recorded and evaluated?

Does every member leaving the employ of your company have the opportunity to discuss in a friendly and frank manner the reasons for the move? And are your staff relations geared to some of the home truths you will hear if this is done?

## 2. The Plan

Having already defined your overall objective and ascertained the facts which are relative to its attainment, you are now in a position to list the specific problems involved in reaching a satisfactory solution. In the case of our expanding company these may include the hostility of the farming community who resent good agricultural land being taken for industrial development; the local schoolteachers whose classrooms are already overcrowded and who dread the prospect of an influx of city-bred pupils who may have a disruptive influence on the minds of the rural children; local householders whose property is near the factory site may fight bitterly against the possible depreciation of the value of their property. All these and many other problems will have to be faced squarely and honestly.

Write down the problems—with the suggested solution and the media which will be employed and see that in a short clear form it is made available to as many members of the staff as are directly concerned at this stage. Public Relations is like a chain and its strength is that of its weakest link. Ignorance on the part of your key staff can be a very weak link indeed.

The more people concerned—and you will find that ultimately everyone connected with your firm will be concerned directly or indirectly—who know what you are trying to do and how you propose doing it—the more likely you are to succeed. Public Relations is the concern of all from the Chairman of the Board to the 'char' who cleans the office floor. The greatest obstacle to effective public relations, internal or external, is ignorance.

Of course you will have to give a good deal more detail to the Board or Chairman or whoever it is you are responsible to—so that they have adequate facts on which to make decisions—including financial appropriations.

If you have got your facts right and produced an intelligent practical programme geared to your organization's needs and resources and have kept those in authority fully in the picture you are more than half way to getting your plans accepted with the means to put them into action.

If you have not done any Public Relations work before remember they will assess your new ideas largely on their opinion of you yourself. So be as efficient as possible—widen your general knowledge—read avidly everything and anything that may help you—go to appropriate evening classes if you can, whatever your age. All these will improve the acceptability of the plans you may put forward. Be tactful and diplomatic and don't step on people's toes. Good Public Relations practice is like planting an acorn, give it time and it will become a solid oak tree and a great strength to the firm. It is possible you may encounter bitter opposition and jealousy. If you do you should regard this as your own personal Public Relations problem, for you've got to learn how to get on with and secure the co-operation of your colleagues. There are some splendid books written on this topic. Books that can help you, such as *To Live*, by Col. du Cann and *Personal Efficiency*, by F. Addington Symonds, both in the *Teach Yourself* series.

You must be prepared for any kind of atmosphere—cordial or chilling. It will be a great advantage to you to know as much as possible about the firm—its history—products—and past record. Sound Public Relations is not a job to be organized by the office boy, and the higher the post occupied by the Public Relations planner the more effective it is likely to be. Best of all is a seat on the Board. Some say that it is difficult to weigh up objectively and also implement policies you yourself have helped to frame. But the advantages of being able to consider these in a Public Relations context at the right time—that is when they are being discussed, usually far outweigh any disadvantages from participation.

To do Public Relations well you should get about and know and discuss your work and theirs with as many people concerned as possible. You will never do really effective Public Relations sitting at your desk the whole time. Get on to the factory or shop floor and get the 'feel' of the firm.

The facts, with your own experience and the experience of others, will enable you to produce a satisfactory plan. But this is only the beginning.

How can Public Relations be evaluated? Before submitting a plan for the approval of top management it should be examined even more carefully than the choice of cloth for a suit—to make sure that it will do what is wanted at the right price.

Glen Perry, assistant director of public relations for E. I. du Pont de Nemours & Company uses the following check questions before presenting a budget for approval or a plan for acceptance.

'ANALYSING A PUBLIC RELATIONS PROJECT'

## Section 'A'

1. What is the objective this project is designed to gain or approach? Is the objective sound and desirable?
2. If the project succeeds will it reach or approach the objective? Are there collateral advantages?

3. Is the project feasible?
    A. Is it reasonable to expect to succeed?
    B. Can it be done with existing personnel?
    C. Does it involve co-operation outside the department?
4. Are there disadvantages to the project?
    A. Is it counter to sound public relations policy?
    B. Is it counter to company policy?
    C. Is the expense too high in relation to possible gain?
    D. Can it embarrass:
        Top management?
        Production?
        Sales?
        Research?
5. How much will it cost?
    Where is the money coming from?
6. In what ways can the project fail?
    What are the foreseeable difficulties?
7. What are the penalties of failure?
    A. Will it embarrass the company if it fails?
    B. Will it embarrass the department if it fails?

*The answer to these questions should add up to the answer to the first question in*

### Section 'B'

1. Why do it at all? Is it worth attempting?
2. Why do it now? Is there any reason for moving fast?
3. Why do it this way? Are there other methods of approach that promise more?

*If it passes all these tests, there are two more questions in*

### Section 'C'

1. Who, if anybody, outside the department must approve the project?

2. Who, if anybody, outside the department must be informed?
   (Courtesy E. I. du Pont de Nemours & Company Inc.)

Appropriations for Public Relations are usually made annually—the size of the budget depending on the size of the job to be done. Public Relations is becoming a key factor in business and more is being spent on it each year. It can be difficult to forecast and budget accurately—but you cannot do effective Public Relations or have them done for you on the cheap. Check your programme along the lines of the test above and if it measures up to what you want, be prepared to pay a reasonable sum for it. Of course your expenditure may vary a great deal depending upon whether you employ your own staff or call upon the services of an outside agency or consultant.

There is a Public Relations Consultants Association, and if you are thinking of employing a consultant you can write to them at 68A Wigmore Street, London W1H 9D1, or phone 01-486-1855, or you can get in touch with the Institute of Public Relations. You should get expert advice on fees and services. The fees will vary from a general retainer to a special fee for a special job—but don't forget that disbursements—especially on things like art work—can be heavy. Remember, too, the general expenses. Many people think of Public Relations as lush living on unlimited expense accounts. Lavish hospitality is always suspect. *Timeo Danaos et dona ferentes.* Moderation and good taste are the factors that count and 'Contacts' that can be fostered only by free entertainment are seldom worth while.

If your organization decides to do its own Public Relations and to appoint one of the staff to direct Public Relations, he must be given adequate staff to enable him to feel free for planning and making contacts with influential

people whose goodwill can in so many ways influence the
attitude of others towards you.

## 3. Action
Next comes the choice of media—the tools—the ways in
which action will be taken.

Nearly every Public Relations project can be undertaken
by the use of almost all media—but in most cases you will
find that one or a combination of a few will produce a good
result.

In any event your choice of media is likely to be limited
by the amount of money which will be allocated for the
plan. Later in this book the various media are dealt with in
detail with suggestions as to their most effective use.

You would be wise to have a clear understanding about
the finance involved—particularly where Public Relations
actively covers the work of other departments, such as
advertising. Many things which are done for other activities
may be charged to Public Relations, and so you should see
that a formula for a fair apportionment is agreed before the
money is spent. This will save a lot of argument later on.
As you remember—the art of administration is the art of
anticipation.

The budget for Public Relations should be realistic. You
just cannot get good results on a shoe string. The sum must
bear some relationship to appropriations for similar functions, such as advertising. Beware of anyone who is prepared
to 'Throw in' Public Relations as an additional service. Such
a make-weight is seldom worth anything at all. Bear in mind
that those in command of your company may have preconceived ideas of what should be done. The Chairman may be
a great believer in films—the Vice-Chairman in television
and so on. All these factors have to be considered.

Above all—never lose sight of the recipient of all this
activity. You must continually put yourself in the place of

the schoolteacher or householder threatened by the new factory and weigh up what really would influence you favourably.

Here we come back to integrity. From time to time you will put up an idea which you think is sound and which is based on your own experience and careful work.

Your Board may overrule you and direct the campaign to take a different form. If your planning work has been done well, you will have gone on record with your recommendations. If the Board's plans don't work out through no fault of yours, the record is there to be read.

But if you are asked to do something dishonest then you have only one course. Protest firmly and courteously. Put your point of view, with integrity, and make it clear that this is a matter of principle. If your views are not accepted —resign. Shed no tears—for a man of character who will do this will not lack opportunities to better himself in a post where his honesty and sincerity will be appreciated.

In planning, thought must be given to the staff who will be directly concerned. Are you to draw on the staff already employed or do you go outside and employ Public Relations consultants? Maybe you will use both. The Institute of Public Relations and the Public Relations Consultants Association are always ready to advise you in a problem like this. The size of the staff depends on the size of the firm, the scope of the plan and the amount of money available.

Secretarial staff should be very intelligent—the work demands a high general standard of education and proved ability to accept responsibility.

Good Public Relations work is an infinite capacity for taking pains. A multitude of details will have to be attended to and you as the planner should learn to and be able to delegate a great deal if you are to supervise effectively and have time to think.

Much of your work will be directly concerned with the giving of information. How this is done is dealt with chiefly in the chapter on relations with the press—but unless this is soundly organized most of your work will be useless.

If you are setting up a Public Relations department, be modest but dignified. Don't overdo lavishness in the office even if the accountants will let you. Remember Cardinal Wolsey and Henry VIII—and Hampton Court Palace!

Get at all costs adequate office equipment. It is difficult to put out an effective press release to the national press in a few minutes on one battered typewriter.

Cutlip and Center in their book *Effective Public Relations*, published by Prentice Hall, put forward the following 'check list for planning'. Well planned programmes should be:

1. *Sincere* in purpose and execution.
2. *Durable* and in keeping with the organization's purpose and character.
3. *Firm*, positive in approach and appeals.
4. *Comprehensive* in scope and continuous in application.
5. *Clear and symbolic*, with simple messages.
6. *Beneficial* to both the sender and receiver of the message.

With your plan should be a timetable for action. Allow ample time—even apparently straightforward jobs like producing a printed poster can take much longer than you think.

Having chosen your media and put your programme into operation—eternal vigilance is now your chief concern. An idea which was splendid one year may not do at all the next.

Every part of your plan must be constantly re-evaluated in the light of experience and achievement.

This is true Public Relations. This is one of the essential differences from mere publicity. From now on you must continually appraise the effectiveness of your operations. Further research is essential and this in turn affects future planning.

And so you see that Public Relations practice is deliberate and sustained—sustained in an effective way because it is based on what others think of your organization as much as it is based on what you think of the public.

# 5 PRESS RELATIONS

Let us now consider press relations as they might be developed by the company putting a factory on the outskirts of a market town and which wishes to explain its point of view to the people already living there. What will be printed in the press, later to be read in many houses in the sleepy, partly hostile community?

What is meant by having something in the paper? Does it mean a 'national newspaper', if so which? for there are quite a number. Or does it mean a 'local newspaper', which may, in certain circumstances, carry more weight certainly on local affairs. And what does it mean when the Board says it would like to have 'something' in the paper? If they are thinking of the local newspaper, does it mean that they are going to take a half-page or a whole-page advertisement announcing the factory project, or are they going to offer a personal interview to the editor so that their views may be made known in that way. Or will an open letter be written to the editor for publication, setting out what they have in mind and the reasons for bringing the factory to the town? Or will they send out press releases? Or will the editor simply be told that there is a good news story and leave it entirely to him or to his reporters to come along and see the plans of the new factory and write it up in any way they see fit? All these are different ways in which the company, if they wish to inform the people in the town about the new factory, can do so by means of the written word as set out in a newspaper. The handling of this kind of activity is not easy to do well. When it is done badly the consequences can be disastrous. Editors of newspapers rightly pride themselves on their independence. Journalists have a code of ethics which they respect—get a copy from the National Union of Journalists or the Institute of Journalists, read it and judge for yourself. Consequently, the story has to be honest, it has to contain facts, it has to be realistic and above all it has to be news. The Board may have fanciful ideas about what the factory will be like and its importance to the community but it is one of the duties of the journalist to cut people down to the right size, not by making them look small, or by inflating or exaggerating but by telling readers the truth, so that they, in turn, may make up their minds about what they have read and form a fair opinion. This is in the true tradition of the press. So, if we are going to use one of, and some say, the most important Public Relations medium—the press—you must understand how it is organized and how it works. You might like to go along to your local library and ask for a book called *Willing's Press Guide*, in the reference section, and look at the list of contents carefully. If you have never seen it before you will be surprised at the number of papers published in this country and, indeed, throughout the world. You will also be quite astonished at the variety of subjects covered by specialist publications. You can read precisely what the Press Council is and does and learn the background to the papers you take yourself. This is one of the first things you should do if you wish to study the workings of the press. The *Teach Yourself* series too has a good book on Journalism by E. Frank Candlin and the Kemsley *Manual of Journalism* is still a classic. Frank Jefkins *Press Relations Practice* (Intertext Books) is also useful.

Briefly, the way in which a newspaper works from the Public Relations point of view is as follows:

The main function of a newspaper is to give news. To get the respect of the press your news has to be accurate and given in good faith. A newspaper man is always working against the clock. You may rather like to be interviewed by a journalist and be quite prepared to spend a couple of hours chatting about this and that but, all the time he is talking to you, machines are waiting possibly for your story and, consequently, if you wish to encourage and foster good relations with the press, remember that you are usually talking to an expert in a hurry. But not in so much of a hurry that he will not take time and care to get his story right; but, having done this, he seldom has the time to linger afterwards. Your relations must be founded on honesty. This is a cardinal principle. If you tell the press the truth they won't let you down. This important point needs some explanation. Now it may be that for reasons best known to himself, the Chairman of the Company does not want the date of the commencement of the building of the factory generally known just yet. At the same time you who are helping him in his Public Relations may be pressed by newspaper men wanting to find out just that one piece of information. It may be that the time will come when you feel that the press ought to know something fairly firm even if they are not at liberty to print it just yet. So you may decide to call a press conference and I will deal in detail with press conferences a little later on. When all the local reporers are together you may say that you wish to make a statement 'off the record'. This means that although you are prepared to give them the story they are not at liberty to print what they have heard—in other words it is confidential at that stage. If more people realized the integrity of journalists and the way in which they will honour this confidence then far fewer people would complain about the press. What you must never do is to speak 'on the record' and say something which perhaps you should not have done and then try to prevent the press man who has quite legitimately got his story from printing it. You may decide to send out a press release with an embargo. That means that you give the time when the press release can go into print. It will not appear before that time if you make your intentions quite clear. This is often important if the press release contains advance details of a speech which is to be delivered. Last minute changes—such as in the choice of speaker if the person billed is taken ill or alterations in the text of the speech to deal with some brand new situation—can be dealt with as they take place.

You should always be available to the press, within reason, and if possible give them the facts accurately and quickly. If you don't know the facts see if you can find out for them and if you are quite unable to discuss a particular matter, say so and if possible give them the reasons for your inability to help. Try to pass them on to someone who can assist. Remember that a reporter is trained to evaluate news. This is accepted with difficulty by many people. What is great news to you may not be news to him at all. The kind of news which an editor will print must make subscribers to his paper feel that they have got their money's worth. It may be a tremendously important event in your firm that a long overdue canteen is to be installed. It may be quite the most important happening in your company since its formation, but you cannot expect it to appear in the headlines of the local newspaper. It is very hard indeed for people to maintain a sense of proportion about this but one should trust the judgement of the press. If there is a story the newspaper men will find it. Give the facts and let them write their stories in their own way. If you are going to give something written to the press in the form of a press release, there are certain golden rules with which you should comply.

First, state very clearly from whom the information is coming; state clearly to whom it is going and whether there is any fixed time when it can be released; put a clear headline at the top showing what it is all about; put a telephone number for day and night calls and an address and, better still, the name of somebody who can give any further information which may be required. Then, in the body of your release, in as few lines as possible, say what, where, when, who, how and why. What the news is. Where it happened. When it happened. To whom it happened. How it happened and why. Don't send out the same press release to all and sundry. Be selective, try and find something suitable for each paper you want to publish your story. Go and see the editors and find out the kind of releases they want and can use. You may be surprised to find out how they vary and at the incredible quantity of articles and releases sent them they discard because they are not submitted in a suitable form. When you are sending out invitations to a press conference don't forget the news agencies. The main ones are:

Press Association; Reuters; Universal News Services; Associated Press; British United Press.

Incidentally, if you have never seen inside a news agency or watched a newspaper being printed write and ask for your name to be included on a suitable occasion when a facility visit is being organized.

If your news is important send it to the B.B.C. and Independent Television News as well. If you follow these rules you have the basis of a good press relations. The basic facts of your story should appear in the first paragraph of your press release. Amplification follows. This enables the busy editor or sub-editor to see at a glance whether your story is worth printing. If it is he may have room only for the first paragraph and if the story isn't there he may not use it at all. If it is a good story and he can make the room he will go on to use the rest of the material contained in the press release. When should you call the members of the press to a press conference? Journalists are busy men and do not relish being summoned to hear something quite trivial. Consequently, one should only call a press conference when you are quite satisfied that it is justified in the first place. It is usually wise to ask all papers likely to be concerned to send a representative. This is sometimes important because favouritism does not go down well with the press. You should honour a story if it has become known to one man first. Press conferences should be held when you have important news to impart, when there are perhaps models or diagrams to be explained and, far more important, when you want to give the members of the press an opportunity of meeting face to face the men making the news and asking their own supplementary questions. The question as to whom you should invite depends on whether the story has a national or local slant and also the type of story. For example, if the company proposes as part of the development to erect in the town a first class swimming bath, then it is unlikely that you would send an invitation to the press conference to the film critics of the local newspapers. This may sound an unlikely event, but it can happen. Make sure that the invitation goes to the people to whom your news is of interest. Before the press men assemble see that the room is large enough, comfortable, with plenty of chairs and tables for them to write on, if possible within easy reach of a number of telephones. It is wise to have a dais or platform so that speakers can be seen and heard clearly. Have plenty of writing material, and if you want to do the thing in style, make up a press kit for them which will contain basic information of use to them in writing their story. The kit would include such items as a personal background of those making the news, a history of the company, the type of product, the parts of the world to which the product is sent, the reasons for the choice of the town and so forth. All this background material, clearly written and concisely stated in hard facts, can be invaluable to a busy press man and will generally ensure that your conference will be adequately covered—provided it is news—and that the reports will be accurate and interesting.

In dealing with press conferences, often one of the most delicate problems is to decide who is going to speak. Frequently this important task is automatically undertaken by the Chairman or the Managing Director, who, although he may be excellent at running a company, may be quite useless in standing up to a barrage of press questions. This again, is one of the problems which has to be faced in Public Relations with diplomacy and tact. Some of the methods by which this situation can be coped with are considered in the chapter on public speaking. It is important that whoever speaks for the company is someone in authority and difficult though it may be, you should try to get the best person available.

What part do you yourself play in all this? It is said that a good Public Relations man like a good child is seen but not heard and you will find that most experienced Public Relations people avoid being on the platform or in front of the camera. This does not mean to say that they do not photograph or speak well, usually they do both with great efficiency, but it is primarily their job to see that the press people come along to listen to somebody they want to hear, somebody from management who is associated directly with the project in hand and who can speak with authority. So you will probably find that the Public Relations officer will prefer to remain in the background and just provide the platform and the occasion for the man best qualified to speak. Often the great man whom the newspaper reporters have come to hear, depends on his Public Relations staff to do research and prepare the material on which he will base his remarks. This may sound curious because you might feel that all great men ought to sit down at their desks and write their speeches themselves. Many do, but as some of you probably realize, even from the brief experience of proposing toasts, such as the health of the bridesmaids at a wedding, that it is not an easy task to prepare a good speech. It takes a lot of time and, consequently busy executives are often forced to depend upon the work done by the Public Relations department in preparing at least the first draft of the speech. Frequently the speech, when finally delivered, bears little resemblance to the one which was first prepared. It may be that only three or four facts remain, but sometimes, if there is a very good understanding between the Public Relations man and his chief, the speech prepared by the former can almost be the finished article.

A good press conference is one that is planned well and the briefing of the speaker with pertinent facts which can be attractively and succinctly presented will do much to ensure success. You must anticipate the type of questions the press are likely to ask, and have sensible and honest replies ready.

You should be absolutely sure of your facts and prepared to substantiate with incontrovertible evidence any statements made by your speaker.

If you are not in a position to make an authoritative statement on any issue be honest and say so. Don't let your speaker wrap things up. The press are experienced and are seldom fooled. It is your job to establish a relationship of trust between the speaker and the reporters. The reputation of a concern in this connection is soon made for good or ill. Once you become known for only calling press conferences to give news or important information honestly and frankly, you will have rendered a signal Public Relations service to your organization.

It is only on rare occasions that a good Public Relations executive would in fact interfere at a Press conference and then only when he felt that disaster was imminent and it did call for his intervention to save the situation. Although as a rule the public relations officer is not automatically a member of the 'platform party' at press conferences and press briefings, there are occasions when he can with great benefit take the chair. To do this, he must be a master of his subject, and able to control a flood of questions in such a way that everyone gets the best possible mileage out of the occasion. On this type of event, it is often easier for the principal speaker to concentrate on answering the questions selected, than to try and run the meeting itself as well. The P.R.O. who can handle this kind of situation skilfully renders a considerable service to his organization and is indeed practising the best kind of public relations in the way in which it should be performed.

What about refreshments? It depends on what the conference is called for and the time of the day. What journalists want is a good story with a human angle—and they want it fast. They do not want to waste time being plied with free drink and food in a protracted carousal ending with a press announcement which is not really news and which is not urgent and which could in any event have been sent out as a press release.

Whatever refreshment is given to the press is unlikely to affect their coverage in any way. Better a good story with nothing than no news with a feast.

Those of you who are not acquainted with Fleet Street may have the impression that the life of a journalist attending press conferences is one long round of parties with unlimited quantities of refreshment, convivial company and a glorious time being had by all. This is not so, the press man has come there for a story. He wants the facts and he wants them fast and if the press conference has been called in connection with something which has given him a good story; then he doesn't want to tarry, glass in hand, chatting to one of the directors while his competitors have already gone to the nearest telephone and are getting their stories filed. This is particularly so in connection with press conferences called in a justifiable emergency.

There are occasions however when a press conference can also be a social function under certain circumstances. For example, if you have called a press conference to look at a new film or a new product which has just been made and the editors concerned are not waiting desperately for their reporters to return with the news about it. This applies usually when the event is to be covered in trade, weekly or monthly papers. Then, under those circumstances, a moderate social occasion can be quite justified.

The time of a press conference is all important. The editor of each paper has tremendous pressure brought to bear upon him during the course of the day with news coming in from all over the world. He has only a limited amount of space within which to put it and a certain amount of that space has, in any event, already been allocated for advertisements. Consequently news from a press conference has to be pretty good to get a place at all in the struggle for space. You should know the times at which the various papers go to print, the times when various editions are printed and, in the light of that knowledge, decide whether you want to try and get your press conference story into the national dailies first thing in the morning or into the London evening and provincial evening papers that night. Pay as much attention to the local press as you do to the nationals.

There is another type of press conference, the holding of which is in fact brought about by the press itself. If a firm has done something, or a government department has taken some action which is hot news—it may well be that the whole press are clamouring for further information and the best thing to do is to act promptly by calling a press conference. Get all the journalists concerned together and deal with their inquiries at the same time, quickly and honestly.

To recapitulate, remember—a press conference is meant

to give genuine news to reporters so don't call one if you can give the news more simply in another way—perhaps by making use of the news agencies, but if the situation is difficult, controversial with many questions to be asked, it is usually best to hold a press conference. Invite to the conference those journalists you know will be interested. If it is a matter of news, then you haven't got time to write letters of invitation, get on the telephone and get the journalists there. Don't promise too much—what you think is a first-class front-page story, may, to the journalists, be quite insignificant. Tell them briefly what it is about and let them make up their own minds. Try and make the press conference informal and don't waste time in getting down to business. Remember, that the first thing a press man wants when he's got his story is a telephone and don't forget to see that there is adequate furniture to write on, with paper. If you have written a press release to go with the conference, see that a copy is on everybody's chair or handed to them as they arrive. It can be read very rapidly by experienced reporters while they are waiting for the meeting to begin and gives them the background they need. Remember you must choose your speaker carefully. He must be someone in authority, he must be able to speak with full knowledge. Bear in mind that the press releases and background material given out are all on the record and so is everything said from the rostrum, unless it is clearly indicated to the press present that the speaker is speaking off the record. You must brief your principal speaker well; see that he has all the essential facts to hand and be nearby in case he requires further information. It pays to be frank. If the proceedings get bogged down or right off the track then, and only then, should you intervene as delicately as possible. Remember that most press conferences are business meetings. It is not a social occasion and there is no need to supply elaborate refreshments. Some do justify a modest party but the occasions when this is so are quite obvious. Pay great attention to the time when your press conference will be held because on that will depend the amount of space, if any, which the newspapers will give you. Don't hold press conferences just for the sake of it otherwise the press will have little faith in you or your activities and cease sending reporters to them. Either provide photographs or allow photographs to be taken if this is justified. Finally, remember that it is often possible where there is a dispute between two groups of people for you to arrange for them to meet together with the press so that an unbiased opinion can be formed of the arguments on either side.

Play the game with the press and you won't be let down. When the press conference has been held you will find that your Board will want to see the coverage obtained in the press. Although it is pleasant to see a story well publicized, sheer weight of press clippings alone do not indicate good Public Relations.

You should if you are going to make use of the press instruct a press cuttings agency to send you the clippings covering your story which they will cut out of such papers and magazines you specify. This is a difficult job and you must not expect an agency to spot everything printed anywhere and in anything about you. Your agency will appreciate receiving your releases.

When you get your press cuttings they should be dealt with promptly and in an efficiently organized manner. A good way is to paste them on to foolscap sheets of paper which are put in an appropriate file and circulated immediately. A list of those by whom they should be seen is put on the outside cover and initialled by each reader before he passes it on to the next person on the list. It should be clearly stated that the file will in any event be collected and passed on to the next reader within a reasonable time whether read or not. Don't let your cuttings languish on one desk when maybe twenty people are waiting for them. If they are all that important have photo copies made for internal use. Some organizations go through all the papers daily and make a short abstract of all the news which may be of interest to senior members of the firm. This Daily News Bulletin draws their attention to items they ought to or might like to read. If they are interested they can send for the full text in the paper itself. In this way management is kept informed of press comment affecting the business. Incidentally, a press briefing differs from a press conference in this way. A press conference usually deals with a specific item of news which is topical. Those attending expect to be able to print a story immediately afterwards. A press briefing, on the other hand, is an opportunity to give the press the background facts, often in considerable depth, so that when the topical story breaks some time later, they are in a position to write about it with authority.

You will probably get many inquiries from the press and your first job as a Public Relations man is to overhaul your information services. Establish quite clearly who is authorized to speak to the press. Arrange day and night telephone manning. If you cannot give an answer at once call back within a reasonable time.

Find out who on each newspaper deals primarily with the matters in which you are interested.

If you are asked to check the accuracy of written copy deal with this as top priority. If you are staging a special event to which the press are invited, see that they are given the facilities they require. Look after them as you would a doctor coming to your house to check the health of your family. They have a job to do and they will want to do it well.

If the press are covering your annual dinner they should be given good seats where they can see and hear the principal speakers, and should be treated in all ways as welcome guests. They should be supplied with refreshment appropriate to the occasion. If the dinner is one where those attending pay for their own wines—see that the press are provided for. They haven't all got unlimited expense accounts.

Try and seat your press men next to people who are good company and who can talk knowledgably about the organization and the function. Attention to details such as these can make all the difference to the way in which the event is reported.

Best of all—have the text of the principal speeches available in advance. This is not always easy to do and sometimes when it is done the reporter will find little he can use. But this kind of planning does show the press clearly that you are making a genuine public relations effort to establish and maintain mutual understanding between your organization and the public.

You don't have to be big to enjoy good press relations. The small firm and the one-man company can on occasion be just as good a source of news. As a typical 'man in the street' you have a part to play. Even if you do not know whether your activities are news or not, getting to know the local reporter is always pleasant and may be very useful. He will be only too pleased to advise you.

*Doing It In Style* (Pergamon) is an excellent book by Leslie Sellers, Production Editor of the *Daily Mail*. In it he says that 'Journalese' is often denigrated, particularly by those incapable of writing lucidly themselves. Some of the criticism is justified, some of the time. But at its best popular newspaper writing is a model of crispness, clarity, conciseness, and immense readability. Let all P.R. people remember this.

Finally—please don't expect an editor to print as news free what should be a paid advertisement.

# 6 HOUSE ORGANS— COMPANY PUBLICATIONS

These are of three types, external, internal and those which combine both functions.

You have all seen the external house magazine. Some of the big companies produce excellent ones, superbly printed on the finest paper, full of most interesting articles with wonderful photographs and although they are expensive to produce, they do much, especially when widely distributed, to enhance the prestige of the company. They are usually sent to shareholders and there are few shareholders who do not feel a glow of pride on receiving some of them.

The internal house magazine is meant for distribution to the employees of the company and, no doubt, some of you have seen these too. They vary even more than the external ones. Some, mainly those which are produced by the bigger companies, are extremely well done. Others are just one sheet, perhaps on duplicated paper which just give details of births, deaths and marriages and moves affecting employees, in other words these merely give the local gossip.

If you are thinking of introducing some Public Relations into your own organization and if it is large enough to merit the regular production of a house organ, then you might well start by considering the questions: 'How do the employers really communicate with the employees? How do they get through to them? How is the relationship between the two continually fostered so that it can be the best that is possible?' In the notes which follow, you may obtain some advice and guidance which will help you to start a house magazine if there isn't one already in existence. Of course, the type of magazine which your organization will agree to publish will depend entirely upon what its purpose is and how much money they are prepared to make available for its publication. A word of warning. It is very difficult to combine the two types of magazines. The prestige magazine, which is widely distributed, will be of very little interest to shareholders of the company or those who are very anxious to know about company policy if it mostly contains details of Nellie's marriage to Tom at the Leicester Branch. In the same way, the employee magazine must be of genuine interest to employees, without concentrating too much on the social scene. They are an ideal way of giving employee-readers hard facts about what the company is, what it is doing and what it stands for as well as telling them briefly about Nellie's marriage to Tom. So in dealing with house organs what you should try to achieve is a well balanced, interesting and informative publication. This is especially necessary in the case of employee magazines. They should help people to feel that they belong to an organization and encourage them to understand and get along with each other better. They should create better understanding all the way along the line carrying items of human interest, family news, news of people's movements, of people who are recovering from illnesses; social events; sports trophy winners and so on. It can carry items about what the management is doing, announcing policy and plans; it can carry special features written by people on the staff—heads of various departments; and it can carry good, short, constructive, accurate articles about the costs and profits, dividends and so on of the organization. You will find, if you are lucky, one or two budding authors in your organization who would be prepared to contribute short articles. It can develop a sense of pride by giving an account of worth-while work done in sections of the company's activities and can carry photographs of the man on the job. It can develop a feeling of loyalty among the employees, e.g. when Joe gets

F

his watch after so many years' service (or maybe something more original than a watch nowadays) then an article on Joe or by Joe is always very well received. It does give the employer a chance to give the man or woman doing a worthwhile job a well deserved pat on the back. Magazines can also carry the off-beat article which will give members fresh interests or make them think about health or safety or ambition. They can also carry comments about some of the great topics of the day. So you see that this is a tremendously interesting field in which the budding Public Relations Officer can, with skill and advice and guidance, do a worthwhile job. Let us now examine these proposals in detail.

Before you rush off and start getting everybody to write something for you so that you can thrust your new-born baby into everyone's hands, sit down and do some very hard thinking, because a good company publication is the result of most careful planning. When considering this particular Public Relations medium the first thing that you have to do is to study the history of your organization. Become familiar with what it does, what it is, what it stands for, how it has grown, how it began, what it is doing at the present time and what its aims for the future are. When you feel that you have a fairly good knowledge about the history of the company, you must, quite obviously, obtain the necessary policy decisions at the highest level on such matters as finance and whether your publication is to be an external or internal one, or a combination of both which is probably more difficult to produce. Take a sheet of paper and write down exactly what you hope to accomplish by a company publication. These are your main objectives. Then decide how you are going to achieve them. Try to imagine the kind of paper you are going to produce. You will probably find it is very much easier to lay down the broad policy governing the production of an external journal than an internal one, but in dealing with the external one you should apply your mind primarily to the circulation. How many people are to receive it? It is surprising how many people can in fact be listed as being eligible but one must be realistic and, although there is a tremendous temptation, if you produce a good company publication, to scatter it around like confetti, it doesn't necessarily mean that it is being read. Incidentally, once you have produced your journal, check from time to time, in the nicest possible way, what your recipients think of it and find out whether indeed they do wish to continue to receive it. Sound organizations go through the list with a tooth comb every year, making certain that the dead wood is cut out and that the journal is being sent only to those people to whom it is worthwhile sending it.

One of the main policy decisions that has to be made in connection with a company publication, which is of the prestige kind, is whether you are going to emphasize what the company does or deal with the sales side of the company's activities. One can readily call to mind some journals where the whole of the space is concentrated on building up a tremendous feeling of pride in what the company does and nowhere is there any pressure put to bear on the reader to buy the product. Once this policy decision is made and you know how many copies you require and the money you have available then you should, as quickly as possible, discuss the matter with an expert—a master printer—who can advise you thoroughly on how to get the best possible value for money.

Dealing with the internal house journal again, the laying down of policy here is much more difficult and you will find that directors and heads of departments often have very decided views as to the extent to which employees can be taken into confidence in connection with company matters. This is a very real problem and if you have permission to start a journal the best way to cope with this kind of difficulty is to produce, initially, a first-class journal which will gain the confidence of management. When this is done you will find that they will probably be more ready to give you worthwhile pieces of information which can properly be passed on to the employees. Remember that the whole object of the exercise is to build up mutual understanding between two groups of people, in this case between the employers on one side and the employees on the other. Having been given the green light to go ahead with a house journal, remember to go into the question of costs very thoroughly. Paper is not cheap these days and even little things like the question of overtime of the person who runs it off on a duplicator all add up.

Once you get your various estimates for having the job done, either on the premises or outside, and you know how much money is going to be allocated to you to do it, the next thing is to find your editor. This should not be as difficult as some people think. It is quite astonishing the number of employees who have got an idea that they can write but this again can be a trap and you should not rush blindly forward and accept the first volunteer, who may be quite unsuitable. The world is full of people who are anxious, willing and ready to help but they are not all budding editors although I need hardly say that your magazine, especially if it is an internal one, will depend to a very large extent on information given to you by other people on the staff. It is also a good idea to get in touch with editors of other house journals and ask them how they started. You will find that their advice will help you enormously in production. Up to a certain level of production you will probably find that you can do it yourself on the premises. If, however, you go beyond the straightforward, duplicated sheet into printing then see that you get the fullest co-operation from your printing department or be advised and guided by a good printer outside.

Once the editor has been chosen and your policy has

been decided, the golden rule is to leave the editor alone to get on with his job. If the editor is going to be you, you will probably appreciate this advice more than anything else I have written. If you fall down on a job, well then the editor is changed, but nothing is more irritating than interference with an editor, who is trying to do his best, by people who really don't understand what he is doing.

Now the next thing is to arrange for the source of your news, information, articles and features. An appeal to all members of the staff for volunteer reporters often produces good results, but something a little more definite is usually required. When you get a list of those who are interested, divide the whole of the staff into sections and see that each reasonably sized section has got a reporter to whom all items of news can be given. See that his name is known to every member of the staff in that section, gradually train them to look at their work and what is happening with a fresh eye and with a view to passing on to their reporter ideas and suggestions so that he can pass them on to you or the editor for selection. Remember that your volunteers are probably going to do a lot of this work for nothing in their spare time so you must encourage them. You will probably find that, initially, there is a tendency for the items of news given to you to be largely of the gossip type, but if you persevere you will find that, as time goes by, the quality and scope will improve. Remember that everyone loves seeing his name in print, so don't, particularly at the beginning, discard almost every offer sent in and fill the journal with your own pet schemes, because this will dishearten those who may have gone to some trouble in presenting their suggestions. You will need great tact, judgement and patience in dealing with your reporters, but once you have got them trained and they feel that it is a team effort to produce the journal, you will encourage a very real sense of devotion and pride. You will probably find that you need about four reporters to each hundred of the staff but this will depend, of course, on how the staff is organized. Small departments, perhaps even of a dozen people who are working on their own, should still have their reporter.

Now what are you going to put in your house journal? I should write down a list of the things you think it should do. Interest. Entertain. Amuse. Instruct. Inform. If you agree that this is what its object is then decide roughly the proportion of space you are going to give in achieving each particular object. Do sit down and do some long term planning. Many house journals seem to have no clear-cut policy from issue to issue, when they could be transformed if the editor would only sit down and plan. For instance, one issue could include a short history of the company to refresh the memories of some of the older members of the staff and enlighten the youngsters. This might be spread over a period of three issues. You may find that you decide to do a series on a particular sport or hobby and that you could get a contribution from a first-class golfer or gardener who will give tips, which will almost run, certainly so far as gardening is concerned, indefinitely.

Now, one very important point. Please remember that you are writing for adults. You are writing for people who are out in the world, making their own way. Over and over again one sees a house journal where the contributions are completely juvenile. Treat your readers as adults and responsible people. Think intelligently and they in turn will think a lot more of your magazine.

Having decided now on the way in which it is going to be done, the next question is on what it is going to be printed. How is it going to appear? There are really three main classes of publication. The best, of course, is the magazine which is nicely printed, nicely bound and which is dignified and distinguished and which is a class job throughout, but this costs a lot of money and is quite beyond the scope of the normal small organization. The next most expensive is the house organ which appears in newspaper style. This is great fun to produce because you will find yourself, unconsciously, trying to reproduce the style and format of your favourite daily newspaper or magazine and this is quite a useful way of tackling the problem. The third is the bulletin. This is usually an A4 sheet which has been duplicated. Each has its place. Each performs a useful function and the format you decide to use will depend, very largely, upon your ability, experience and skill and above all, on the amount of money available for its production.

The means by which the magazine is produced can, of course, vary from first class printing down to ordinary typing. Most of you will probably start with typing because it is easy to do and can be done readily on the premises, but it has great limitations particularly so far as the question of illustrations and photographs is concerned.

Now comes the final problem. Having got your magazine ready, how will you distribute it? If it is a good journal many companies like to send it by post to their employees' private addresses so that when it arrives in the morning it does, literally, become a family magazine and everybody in the house reads it. This, of course, adds greatly to the cost of production but it is estimated that, of the internal house journals produced, well over half are read, in fact, by members of the firms' families. Most journals are, however, distributed manually on a departmental basis.

So there it is. Of all the Public Relations opportunities which you may like to try this is probably the one which may seem the easiest, but remember to discuss the project thoroughly with everybody who matters, particularly the Board of Directors and Personnel Officer. Get everyone interested and settle policy and all the major issues which are likely to create friction right at the start before you go into print. If you do this, plan the production well, enlist the support and organize the method of receiving news, and distribution, then you will look back with pride on a very worthwhile achievement in the field of Public Relations in your organization. Even if you have only a few employees a 'News Sheet' put up on the notice board regularly would probably be well worth while. Of course, if you are able to make modest payments to your contributors, so much the better.

I have quite deliberately not dealt with the technique of printing. This is a highly specialized craft and one of which Public Relations makes considerable use. Find a good printer and be advised by him. You will learn a great deal and he will be only too pleased to help in the choice of type, layout and so on. The British Association of Industrial Editors are very helpful. Consult them too.

# 7 THE SPOKEN WORD—SPEECHES—TALKS—DISCUSSIONS

One Public Relations medium which everyone has, is the ability to speak, some well and some badly, and this is one of the assets of your organization or yourself which can be developed into a very powerful implement indeed.

There are a number of books written about the technique of public speaking. *Teach Yourself Public Speaking*, by P. Westland, is good and there are courses arranged, some by local authorities and some by private enterprise at which public speaking is taught. To what use can the spoken word be put effectively in Public Relations ? Just think for a moment of some of the situations in which you may have found yourself during the past few months. Perhaps you attended a dinner at which a number of after-dinner speeches were delivered. What were they like ? Probably all too few good ones, some indifferent and a number quite bad. Some speakers perform with a sense of duty, some with very little application to the occasion and some give nothing more than a collection of old stories strung together. You may go to business conferences, meetings of departmental heads, staff association meetings at which ideas are put forward for acceptance and action. You probably know who are the speakers you like listening to and those you consider better than others so begin to study, seriously, their techniques, how they put their views across, and how they gain acceptance for the ideas they speak about. If you remember that the whole object of Public Relations is to establish and maintain mutual understanding then, obviously, when people meet and talk to each other, this is the most natural way in the world of creating, improving and maintaining a good understanding. Don't just think of public speaking as being the great occasion, the once a year event at which the outstanding personality occupies the platform. Applied intelligently, the public relations activity of speaking can be used daily in many other different ways—let me give you some examples.

The other day, a number of sales representatives were holding their annual meeting after a particularly bad year. Instead of receiving the usual pep talk from the Chairman, to their delight and astonishment when the party assembled in the conference hall they found a small stage and as soon as they were seated a playlet was put on for them which showed, in humorous terms, that the management had appreciated the difficulties they had encountered during the past year. At the end of this the audience was addressed, quite shortly, by the Sales Manager who gave them a word of encouragement and so a new year started with their being in good heart and ready to tackle their work with fresh enthusiasm. Now this was speaking with a difference. The sales representatives knew the Manager was going to speak to them. They expected the usual kind of pep talk given on these occasions. And indeed the Sales Manager *did* speak to them. Shortly and effectively—after others had spoken the words he had written for the playlet which showed clearly he understood their difficulties. And so the spoken word on this occasion was convincing and inspiring.

Again, every time someone contacts you in connection with your business and you talk to him about it he is weighing it up by the way you talk and what you say. This is particularly true of receptionists and telephonists and it is probable that the spoken word uttered by them has as much effect on the reputation of an organization as anything else that the company does.

Have you ever been away from the office—wanting to

contact it—and an energetic and kindly host says—'I'll get them for you'—with results from your own switchboard which make you hang your head in shame.

Don't blame the operator. Blame yourself. What have you ever done to make her feel she is really important to the firm? Has she ever been round it? Are there some flowers to lighten her tedious task? Does she really *know* what each person who is merely an extension number to her—actually does? If not you have some staff Public Relations to put in hand at once—to improve the impression given by the spoken word to anyone contacting you or your organization.

Another way in which the spoken word is effectively employed, which is beginning to supersede, in many cases, the straight lecture, is the panel discussion. Properly handled this is a delight. Getting together two or three first-class speakers, limiting them to a set time in which to impart their views and then discussing matters of moment between themselves can often teach an audience more with enjoyment and interest than listening to one man talking for the same length of time. Again, a question and answer discussion with plenty of participation from the audience is always a good method of putting across ideas to the public. When you make arrangements for talks of different kinds do give opportunities for questions 'from the floor'. It makes for a better talk with greater impact and much more pleasure for the audience if plenty of time is given for them to take part. It is often better to cut speaking time to a minimum and to allow more time for questions afterwards. However in order to get that kind of response from the audience, the initial remarks have to be interesting, stimulating and sometimes provocative. A very good way to start a 'question and answer discussion' of this kind is to commence by posing a number of questions which you think will interest your audience. You then deal in detail with perhaps only some of them and leave the rest for questions, if they have aroused the interest of your audience, at the end of your address. Again, at conferences of all kinds, the spoken word naturally plays a vital part. There we have the straight lecture or address which, in the hands of the right person, can be a joy; but which so often leaves one with the impression that although the speaker knows a great deal about his subject he doesn't quite know how to put it across. Finally, demonstrations are important too. One is often taken to look at a piece of machinery, or a process, which of itself seems to be quite interesting. Sometimes it is explained lucidly and in a way one remembers, but all too often one is overwhelmed with a mass of statistics and technical jargon which one has great difficulty in understanding and one feels that another opportunity has been lost to take advantage of the spoken word.

If you are going to consider public speaking in your firm, the first thing to do is to list the opportunities and the occasions, on which you think the spoken word will be important. List your audiences. List clearly, as far as you can in advance, the topics upon which your audiences will expect to hear something. Prepare, say, a year's programme to start with and then turn your attention to the question of who will be the best person to speak on each occasion. This can present difficulties. The Chairman or the Managing Director or a senior official perhaps will feel *they* ought to speak; but it doesn't always follow that they are the best persons to do so. Drawing up the list of speakers calls for great diplomacy, tact and skill. If you do public relations effectively it can be so arranged that your dignatory takes the Chair, content to conduct the proceedings with brevity, but allows the star speaker to actually deliver the address.

The ideal way to organize speaking is to set up a Speakers' Bureau. This can be quite an extensive operation, depending, of course, on the scale of your plan and resources. The simplest method is to list all your speakers on a card index with details of what they can speak about and where they are prepared to speak; with sufficient information to enable you to pick the right speaker for the right locality at very short notice. If you operate on a national scale you will, of course, cross index by localities in which your speakers reside. Let us take as an example a firm employing say a considerable number of people. The basic operation will be to recruit your speakers, train them if necessary, help them prepare their speeches, see that they are given the opportunity to speak, arrange the details for their appearances, give them any equipment they may require to enable them to speak effectively and see that their speeches get the publicity they deserve in the appropriate places. The appropriate place for publicity may be a local or national newspaper, trade journal, staff magazine or notice board.

Now, about recruiting speakers. You may find that you already have a number of good, experienced, speakers on the staff who naturally take their place in the Speakers' Bureau but that you have not got enough to launch an effective and far-reaching campaign. A surprising number of people welcome an opportunity of learning to speak in public and you may find that if you offer courses in public speaking to all the employees, which can be arranged quite easily, you may be astonished at the talent you have available unknown in your own firm. Having given all an opportunity to speak and having selected those who are going to do so on behalf of your company the next steps are:

1. To train your selected speakers to speak properly.

2. To train them to speak effectively about your company and its affairs.

You may have a member of your staff who is a very good speaker indeed, but, he may not be trained to speak about your company in the way it should be. This will be one of your jobs, to see that this is done. You should encourage those who have the talent and who are really keen on learning to speak in public.

Ask your most experienced speakers to give talks on the subject. Encourage the students to listen to themselves on tape recordings and to persevere although they may be upset the first time they hear their own voices.

Encourage those who wish to attend night school lectures and see that they have suitable helpful easy textbooks. If you have a sufficient number, run a course for groups of employees by inviting an expert lecturer to instruct your students. Put debates and discussions on the programme of social activities.

Having got your speakers, what about your speeches?

Some people like to write their own, others expect their talks and addresses to be written for them but in any event what you should do if you are running a Speakers' Bureau is to know fairly accurately what your speakers are saying, wherever they may be and whatever audience they are addressing. This means skilful preparation. Some people like to write out their speeches in full, others prefer to speak from short notes or even three or four lines scribbled on the back of a postcard.

If it is one of your tasks to see that those who speak for your organization speak well, you should clear with them a set form of speech, in outline, which deals with all the salient points to be put across and these points will, of course, have been settled from a Public Relations point of view and will form part, as already explained, of a Public Relations plan which has a specific objective. If, for example, the object of your overall plan is to increase the esteem in which your organization is held, or the reputation of your organization as employers, then in checking speech material you will see that a proper proportion of the speech deals with what your organization is doing by way of serving the community, or by improving relations with employees. Here let me sound a word of warning. Audiences are extraordinarily perceptive and a speech must tell the truth. If you have done something worthwhile, the speech is one of the best ways of publicizing it but no speech or any other Public Relations activity should be used in covering up a failure or giving half truths or concealing the truth. Attempts to do this usually result in the audience seeing through the manoeuvre at once, being alienated and the speaker losing a great deal of goodwill which he may have had before. So know thoroughly what your speakers are going to speak about. Try and have a fairly wide variety of topics on which talks can be given. If a little thought is given to this, it is quite astonishing, in any factory, one making, say, broom handles, how many topics for talks can emerge. The kinds of wood, the machining processes, sales, staff relations, the list is endless, but choose those which are really going to be of interest to your audience.

Now, you will probably be asked for guidance about the preparation of a speech. The first thing is to get into the jackdaw habit; every time you see a newspaper paragraph which contains a germ of an idea, clip it out and paste it in a book or on a card or just put the clipping in an envelope. Index your clippings with adequate cross-references and file them. Gather information all the time even on subjects which seem remote from your organization, have good books of reference handy or make intelligent use of the public library. Tell the librarian what you are doing and enlist his aid. Write to organizations which deal with the topics in which you are interested. You will find all sorts of people wonderfully helpful once they know you are seriously interested in getting material of this kind, and you will make some good friends. Study the trade journals. You should, without a great deal of trouble, be able to produce proper background information for any speech which your organization might feel should be delivered.

Next, you should have as much information as possible about the audience. It is quite unforgivable to launch a speaker into a situation where he speaks to an audience of a kind, sex or age, for which he was totally unprepared. You can easily find out what the audience is likely to be and let your speaker have details about it in good time.

In preparing a speech you should list precisely what your objectives are, what you hope people will tell those who could not come or who may arrive late and ask 'What did he say'. If you write down the answer you would like them to give and make that the central theme of a speech then you are more than half way to ensuring that a good address is going to be delivered. Having decided on your objectives, you then decide how you are going to reach them. Are you going to reach them by amusing your audience, shocking them, intriguing them, frightening them, instructing them, entertaining them ? Know the facts and, wherever possible, have some which can be used with light relief so that one does not listen throughout to a very heavy stolid speech.

Work out a plan for the speech which is sensible and lively. Bear in mind the amount of time which will be available for its delivery. Have a good opening. The commencement of a speech today is quite unconsciously being compared by all listeners with the start of television or radio programmes. Whereas in the privacy of their own homes they can walk across and switch the set off, with a speech they usually have to stay there and listen, but, mentally, they switch themselves off and, therefore, it is absolutely vital that the speaker captures the attention of his audience as soon as he gets on his feet and starts talking. Never, never, never apologize for speaking. Please don't get up and say: 'I do not know why I have been called upon to say these few words when there are so many people in the room more qualified than I to do so.' The only result of such an opening is that inwardly nearly all your audience will be saying to themselves 'Hear, hear. Why does he do it?'

Having settled on the opening, draft out the main points which have to be made and then pass the result of your efforts to your speaker. He may decide to write the final speech himself, pass it back for you to write the whole thing or be quite content to speak on the few notes which you have done.

Take some trouble over the title for a speech. This is well worthwhile but it can be a difficult problem. The speech may be about a piece of equipment with a name which is not particularly attractive but which does perform a function interesting to a non-technical audience. Use your ingenuity. Think out the human angle and, with a little care, you will come up with a title which will be honest, arresting, interesting and which will attract an audience to come along and hear it. You must be honest about this. Never mislead your audience with your title. There is a story of the speaker who was going to speak about 'the Land of the Redskins' to a juvenile audience who thought they were going to hear about 'Cowboys and Indians' but, in fact, what he wanted to speak to them about was how the boys and girls could learn to grow tomatoes in their own plots in the garden. So far as the end of speech is concerned always finish on a strong note.

It was once said that the best speech of all is made like this: The speaker gets up and tells his audience what he is going to tell them; he then tells them and then tells them what he has told them! Do bear in mind this third part. The audience usually don't know the subject as well as the speaker. They do like to be reminded about what they have heard, provided the reminding comes in a strong finish and draws together all the themes which have been developed by the speaker. So get a stong ending, recap very briefly what the audience has been told and finish on a strong note.

G

Have a very clear idea of what you want your audience to be thinking when they leave after listening to the speech. You may want them to do something. You may want them to take some action as a result of the speech. Then, tell them at the end precisely what they are asked to do. If you have stated the case well and it is a good case some may go out and do it. Over and over again you will hear quite good speeches which were really a call to action, but they faded away at the end and the audience ambled out and nobody did anything at all. So, coming back to objectives, if you want the audience to do something as a result of the talk, then see that it is included, quite categorically, and quite specifically, in a strong ending.

If you are running a Speakers' Bureau you should also give attention to the preparation of speakers' guides or notes. Many organizations have prepared excellent ones. Try and find an organization which has a bureau and notes and see if the person in charge would be prepared to let you see them. It is wise to keep your speakers' notes on a loose leaf system because as facts and statistics change so the latest information can be put in without difficulty. Don't try and make the speakers' notes speeches in themselves. Do separate short notes on a large number of points so that any combination of them can be used by speakers in dealing with particular aspects. Be honest in your notes and try and anticipate the difficulties with which your speakers are going to be confronted. One section should be entitled 'Honest Answers to Awkward Questions'. Have another section 'Vital Statistics' and another dealing with 'Press Comments' about the subjects with which you are dealing. Another one can be on 'Quotations' and so on; the list is endless. It is of the greatest possible assistance for a speaker to have comprehensive notes not only to refer to at the time he is delivering the speech, if he so desires, but which he can read quietly beforehand and which will arm him for any of the awkward points which may arise at the end of his talk or discussion. He will then not be left floundering and wondering why he wasn't told that this kind of thing was likely to happen. Above all, your notes must be prepared with integrity because the speakers must speak with sincerity knowing they can rely upon your giving them completely accurate and unbiased factual information.

Having set up your bureau and having your speakers adequately prepared you now are ready to consider obtaining speaking engagements for them. This is very much easier than you might expect. If your speakers are good, you will find that news of a competent speaker travels fast and far from being unable to find platforms upon which the speakers can deliver their talks you may find you are overwhelmed with requests for your speakers to go here, there and everywhere.

This calls for great care and you should see that your star speakers are not swamped with speaking engagements. There are usually many platforms available for the speakers and consequently it is almost essential for you to decide in good time the types of audiences you want to reach and the sections of the community to whom you wish to speak. There are, of course, groups in every society who may be described as influence-formers and you may wish to make arrangements for your speakers to talk to them. People like school-teachers, professional bodies, Rotarians and so forth. If you wish to know the opportunities for speakers in these circles, your best plan is to write to the secretary of the local branch of the national organization. The address is usually in the telephone directory. *Whitaker's Almanack* is an invaluable source of information. Or you can contact the national headquarters of the organization concerned, telling them that you have speakers available on certain subjects and asking for the name of the local organizer so that you can get in touch with him. If you know the local organizer already

so much the better. Ask the local secretary of the organization the kind of talks they like and supply the need if you can.

When you are offering to provide a speaker let the intended audience, or at least the secretary of the organization
to whom you propose sending him know something about
him. Get each of your speakers to supply you with short
adequate biographical notes setting out what his background
is. This will enable the secretary to invite him with confidence and enable him to be introduced properly, effectively
and in an interesting manner to the audience. Some organizations also like to receive a photograph of the speaker as
well so this is always a useful thing to have available. In
making arrangements for the speaker, come to a clear
understanding as to whether any expenses are to be paid or
not; whether hospitality or accommodation is to be provided; what time they want the speaker to arrive; who is
going to meet him; what transport arrangements are to be
made; precisely how long he is expected to speak; are there
going to be questions afterwards; and is the press going to
be present. Often you will find that a speaker will say one or
two things, either flippantly or confidentially quite unaware
that the press are present and it is unforgivable for him to
try and retract what he has said. The press have their own
standards of integrity and, if the press have been invited to a
meeting, unless it has been clearly put to them that what the
speaker is saying is 'off the record' then they are entitled to
report what they have heard. Do get that point quite clear,
and see that all the speakers know it. If the press are present
and if your speaker then does want to say something confidentially he must make it clear that he is speaking 'off the
record' to prevent it from being reported. If you are seeking
press coverage for your talk, it is wise to send an advance
extract from the talk or the full text to the local papers with
an embargo that it is not to be published until after the talk
has been delivered. If this is done corrections can be made

in the text on delivery and the newspapers then have an accurate account of what transpired to use if they so wish.

Richard Darrow of Chicago in the Dartnell Public Relations Handbook gives a good check list which you can use yourself if you are arranging speaking engagements or send to your hosts if you have been invited to talk, and they haven't given you the required information already. Here is an expanded version:

1. Do you approve the title .............. suggested for my talk on ........ 19.. at ................?
2. How many minutes are allotted to my talk?
3. At what time do I appear on the programme?
4. At what time do I meet my escort if any and where?
5. Who will the escort be?
6. How will I identify him?
7. Or do you prefer that I arrive alone?
8. When do you wish me to appear at the meeting?
9. Who will be the chairman?
10. Will the chairman introduce me?
11. When will I meet the chairman?
12. If the chairman does not introduce me, who will?
13. May I have an advance copy of the programme for this meeting as a guide to other subjects and speakers?
14. May I have a copy of your season's programme to see what other speakers you have had and their topics?
15. If the original plans change, how will I be notified?
16. Who will be in the audience? (i.e. men, women, or both, adults, juniors, professional people, experts, just members, visitors, V.I.P's, etc.)
17. Will the press be present?
18. Who will prepare and release publicity?
19. May I see the copy to be released?
20. Other guests at the speaker's table or platform?

21. Will there be . . . lectern . . . speaker's light . . . blackboard . . . epidiascope . . . screen . . . projector?
22. Will a question period follow the talk?
23. What questions are most likely to be asked?
24. Following the meeting, do I remain?
25. Will the attached biography and photograph be sufficient for your needs?
26. If a stay overnight is indicated, where will I stay and at whose expense?
27. If the venue is difficult to find do you issue a map to assist visitors?
28. What are the most convenient train times?
29. Are there adequate parking facilities?

This check list can be adapted or amended to meet almost any occasion. Its use can avoid many difficulties and most important matters can be tactfully dealt with in a businesslike way at the right time, that is in good time before the event.

When the talk has been given you should keep records showing whether it has been worthwhile. A good idea is to prepare a formal report card upon which the returning speaker will indicate the number, sex and type of audience, the manner in which his talk appeared to have been received, the kind of questions put to him afterwards and so on, gathering material which will be useful to you in planning the activities of your Speakers' Bureau and making it more effective as time goes by.

The larger the organization the more obvious the opportunities for speaking appear to be. But everyone can improve his own personal public relations or that of his firm, however small, by becoming a good speaker. Indeed you will find that some of the best come from 'one man' concerns.

# 8 RADIO AND TELEVISION

Of all the media available for public relations, radio and television are the ones with the widest influence. Most of sound radio in England, Wales, Scotland and Northern Ireland is provided by the British Broadcasting Corporation operating with National and Local programmes. Commercial radio is chiefly received from Radio Luxemburg. In addition the B.B.C. do a great deal of broadcasting to audiences outside the United Kingdom by means of the European and Overseas Services. Full details of the organization of the B.B.C. can be obtained from the B.B.C. Handbook which is published annually. This is an essential reference work if you contemplate participating in B.B.C. programmes either for sound or vision. With the advent of the popular priced transistor radio, and the ever increasing development of V.H.F. local stations, sound broadcasting has been given a new lease of life and statistics show that the majority of the population listen in some of the time during each day. Radio has become part of the British way of life. It exercises a powerful influence on its audience and can give unrivalled opportunities for good public relations chiefly in two ways—news and features. Many people, regardless of the papers they take, rely upon news broadcasts to give them the latest information. The radio will always be more topical because broadcasting reporting is right up to the minute whereas papers have to be produced and distributed and this takes time.

If you have never been over a sound radio station you should endeavour to do so and see for yourself how news is gathered, sifted, selected and broadcast.

The press agencies' material is usually received by the B.B.C. and used where appropriate but because of the strictness of the rules against advertising it is only in wholly justifiable circumstances that the name of a firm or product will ever be mentioned on the air.

Nevertheless if you think you have a good news story you should release it to the B.B.C. in the same way that you make it available to the press. If it does not form part of the 'National News' it may still find a place in the local news broadcasts. More time is being given to local news. You should, however, remember that by radio, news is *heard* and this often calls for a quite different method of presentation from that prepared for the press. Quite apart from submitting news items to the B.B.C., if your organization is concerned in a project which is sufficiently important—such as a royal visit, the B.B.C. may send along its own reporters to cover the event. This calls for thorough planning and meticulous time keeping. Make early contact with the officials concerned at the B.B.C. and be guided by their vast experience. One of the the best articles ever written on 'Royal Visits' is that by Charles Hervey, formerly of the United Steel Companies Ltd., and published in the quarterly Journal of the Institute of Public Relations.

If your firm is a large one with considerable resources and overseas interests you may have facilities which the B.B.C. might like to make use of on suitable occasions as a background to the news.

If a 'trouble spot' develops overseas and becomes news and a member of your staff who is an authority on the place has just returned to this country from it, he may be just the man wanted to tell listeners the background details they would like to hear.

Weigh up the various activities of your concern—assess their news potential—get into touch with the B.B.C. and find out in good time whether they are likely to be interested in any news you may have from time to time and if so what, how, and when they would like it.

Don't overlook tape recordings. The B.B.C. have a highly skilled staff who will visit your firm for a 'news interview' recording session if suitable material is available and in certain circumstances they may use tapes done by you provided they measure up to the very high technical standards of the B.B.C.

So much for news—now what about features? These can be so varied and programme planners are always on the look out for new, good and interesting material.

If you have something you think may interest the B.B.C. you should send twelve copies of it to them, marking one for the producer of the programme you believe most suitable for its use. The facility department will circulate your suggestions to all sections which might consider it.

Features and ideas for features must be well written—contain intelligent thoughts—must have substance which will appeal to the listener—must deal with the topic in the right way—and if you are to provide speakers, then those who are to broadcast must be up to the job. Listen as much as you can to programmes which may offer you opportunities but don't rush off and submit exactly the same ideas.

You should have a clear idea as to what your feature is designed to do. Is it to amuse, entertain, inform, instruct, educate—provoke? To what extent do you expect it to be broadcast—nationally—locally? Is there anything like it already being broadcast? How often is it to be broadcast—how long will it be—will it form part of a series or is it a single broadcast?

You should have sound answers to all these questions when you approach the B.B.C.

Whatever you do, don't forget research. You must be absolutely sure of all your facts, and prepared to quote chapter and verse. If a mistake is made it may be heard by millions of people and you will be surprised at the number who seem to take a fiendish glee in writing in to the B.B.C. drawing attention to an error!

You may also have to do some 'audience research'; finding out the time and type of programme most likely to be interesting. The B.B.C. run an elaborate audience survey department whose help and guidance you should endeavour to obtain. You should certainly study the reports and remember that a good deal of listening is done by women at home during the daytime—and this offers specialist fields of many kinds dealing with topics of interest to them. In the evening, programmes are usually much more widely based on the family as a listening unit.

A good microphone manner is usually acquired by prac-tice, for there are very few natural broadcasters. Familiarity with modern tape recording can go some way in preparing those who may be called upon to speak on the air. If you have to prepare what is to be broadcast by a member of your organization, remember to write clearly and concisely just as though you were talking to a group of friends around a table. You should endeavour to avoid long words and involved sentences. It may be difficult for you to produce copy of the exact length required, so you should time it, on a tape recorder if possible. Get a colleague to listen to it as though it were a broadcast, and in this way you should be able to produce what is wanted, provided the basic material is good.

Features can be used in all sorts of ways—as straight talks by people qualified to speak—actual broadcasts of events which are happening—interviews of all kinds—musical or dramatic programmes—unscripted discussions—quizzes—debates—or programmes with invited audiences who will be expected to participate in the broadcast.

Check through the many types of programme on the air and see if you have something to contribute to any of them.

Events in your organization—stories, incidents, facts—anything with a 'human angle' will always be given careful consideration by those in charge of programmes.

If you write a script—write on one side of the paper—double-space it—use paper which will not rustle and put distinguishing marks for emphasis and pauses. You must start off with something to hold the interest—remember there may be thousands listening ready to turn off the programme if it doesn't capture their attention at once. It's your job to produce something so good they will stay with you. Remember they can only *hear* you. You must describe vividly if you want them to see and feel. Be careful not to bore with bare facts and avoid too many statistics. Be conversational and above all be sincere.

Much of what has been said about radio is applicable to television but here there are two networks to consider. The B.B.C. and the Independent Contractors.

The Independent Television Authority set up in 1954 controls privately financed companies who supply the programmes. Advertisers pay the programme companies for time during which the advertisement can be televised.

Virtually the whole of the country is now covered by programmes transmitted by companies in various areas, the chief of which are Anglia, Associated Television, Border, Channel, Grampian, Granada, Harlech, London Weekend, Scottish, Southern, Thames, Tyne Tees, Westward Ulster and Yorkshire. The Independent Television News Ltd. provides a news service for all programme companies.

Most television programmes are of the following types: sports programmes, variety shows, shows in which the audience participates, drama, and films of various kinds including documentaries—and, of course, news coverage.

So far as public relations activities are concerned, television offers, in specific fields, the greatest opportunities of all. The two main types are commercial and non-commercial.

So far as commercial television is concerned this is primarily a matter for an advertising department or agency. Nevertheless you should be familiar with the whole process of production and presentation and if you are not and have no opportunity, get into touch with a leading advertising agency and ask them to allow you a facility visit to their firm. The quality and effectiveness of the advertisements appearing on television vary tremendously. But whatever their sales appeal, good Public Relations is the 'plus factor' in all excellent advertisements. Ask the essential questions—'Does this establish and maintain mutual understanding between the organization and its public?' If it does it is good Public Relations. Study the 'commercials' carefully and analyse the ones that appeal to you. You will probably find they are based on simplicity and sincerity with first-class technical production.

The relationship between Public Relations and advertising is a delicate one; sometimes the division between them is quite clear while at others it is tenuous. It can be validly said that much of advertising is publicity and publicity is one of the adjuncts of Public Relations. The more those dealing with advertising understand Public Relations and vice versa the better for all concerned.

Dealing with non-commercial television on both B.B.C. and I.T.V., the main opportunities will be by way of news and features. These may either be used by the network whereby a programme is transmitted by all or a number of the programme contractors or it may be used locally only. Local programmes endeavour to maintain the same high technical standard of the national networks. You must remember that in television, news narration and films are closely linked. You must 'see what you hear'.

How do you get an item accepted by your local TV station? Once again, go and see them. Find out how they work. Ask for a facility visit. Meet the News Editor, the programme planners and producers—but remember they are very busy men indeed and seldom have time for casual callers. You may have to wait some months but it will be well worthwhile. Write in and request a convenient appointment. If you want to see a B.B.C. programme, write to the Ticket Unit, B.B.C., Portland Place, London W.1. If it is an Independent Television production you should write to the individual contractor.

If you have a news story which you think is likely to be of interest to television don't over-value it. Don't promise the news editor something wonderful and come up with something insignificant. Find out what appeals and work to his standards. Once trust and confidence are established they will be more likely to accept what you say. Your news should be 'newsworthy' in the widest possible sense. Not just news to your concern but of genuine news interest to the public at large. Don't be afraid of controversial topics. If you have an intelligent and well-informed management and your public relations is in good shape they should never shirk the opportunity for honest comment on a matter of public interest. Trade union leaders are usually quite ready to express their views and the reluctance of business leaders to do the same is from time to time hard to understand.

One recent development has been the production of a number of programmes which can only be called 'Trial by Television'. Sometimes these can do much good by exposing a matter to the full glare of publicity in the public interest. There are other occasions however when the producer seems to be primarily concerned with controversy. If you are asked to participate in any programme you should get it absolutely clear whether it is going to be done live or taped. If it is taped you will have virtually no control whatsoever over the final programme as transmitted. You or your chief may give a half-hour interview only to find that your contribution in the end amounts to forty-five seconds in which a few statements are taken from their context, in your view, with unsatisfactory results. If it is done live you may expect to give a talk by yourself or have a discussion with one or two other people, but on arrival at the studio you can find to your surprise that you are confronted with a dozen of your biggest and most vociferous critics. By all means participate in television programmes and take all reasonable opportunities of putting your point of view. But do go into this media with your eyes wide open. And don't be afraid to decline an invitation.

Many firms and organizations have facilities which are useful to television producers. Big national institutions like the Port of London Authority get scores of requests for filming facilities on the Thames, in warehouses, docks, wharves and so on. Give all the help you can. If it happens, it is wise to have a form of contract and indemnity in case anything untoward happens during the television production. By working with the camera teams you will get a useful insight into the problems and techniques of making a good programme.

It is in the field of comment and interview on television that public relations can come into its own, but remember that the cameras are the supreme exposers of subterfuge and dishonesty. Alternatively, no other medium offers greater opportunities for sincerity and integrity.

Consider all the activities in which your company is engaged and list those which you think may have a news or feature value on television and submit brief details *as far in advance* as possible as programmes are often planned months ahead.

Remember too that a TV screen is quite small and that it just does not have the same scope as a cinema screen. On the other hand if you are making a documentary or news film bear in mind its television potential. If it is of interest to the television companies, co-operate with them at an early stage giving plenty of time for slight alterations of a technical nature which could well result in your documentary film appearing on television and to a much wider audience in a much shorter space of time.

If members of your organization are going to be televised make sure they know what to wear. A good Public Relations man clears this at an early date with the Producer. The spread of colour television has added a new dimension to viewing and to public relations. All your television concepts have to be revised and reassessed if you are dealing with colour. The people you put on the programme, the clothes they wear and so on.

And don't forget closed-circuit television. You can buy your own equipment or hire a company who will shoot an event and relay it live over special lines to an audience somewhere else. This is often done when more people want to attend a meeting than can get into the hall, and the unlucky (or lucky) ones see and hear the great man elsewhere on closed-circuit TV. It can be expensive. But it has great potential, for bringing people far apart together, and can be well worth while. Another refinement is TV projection of a speaker on to a huge screen behind him while he is actually speaking. The Institute of Directors do this very successfully at their annual meeting at the Albert Hall. Be careful though . . . it enables those in the balcony to see every wart!

There are two good books on writing for television from which you can learn a great deal. The first is *Writing for Television*, by Arthur Swinson, published by Adam and Charles Black, and the other is *Profitable Scriptwriting for TV and Radio*, by Gale Pedrick, published by C. Arthur Pearson, Ltd. Even if you do not intend to do any writing yourself you will learn a great deal about television production which will be most useful in your dealing with this medium. Arthur Swinson lists the difficulties of television compared with sound radio, the film and the theatre, and it certainly has qualities all of its own—a sense of immediacy —a sense of reality close to the reality of life as it is known to the mass of the people. It is not merely a substitute for the theatre or cinema which holds a mirror up to life; it is rather an open window on life itself.

One of the many useful tips given by Gale Pedrick deals with the search for material. He calls it 'The elusive idea' and writes 'I beg from the depths of grim experience not to lose a good idea or even a useful phrase because you are disinclined (I mean too lazy, of course!) to write it down. Is there anything more maddening than to try and recall some flash of inspiration only to find it eluding you? One can lie awake for hours trying to grasp again those mental will-o'-the wisps. How one begrudges the precious time lost as one stares at a too-hastily squiggled note on the back of an envelope, a visiting card or a bus ticket. A tiny effort of will and all that frustration would have been avoided.

'No really good idea need ever be lost. Take the trouble, therefore, to make notes of every promising thought. You won't regret it. An opening phrase—a story outline—the subject for an entertaining talk. Don't lose them. More than that, having hatched out these themes and noted them down—act on them without delay.'

Finally it doesn't matter whether you are a tycoon or in business on your own account. You can still get a good idea which may be heard and seen by millions.

# 9 FILMS

One of the main ways in which Public Relations is performed is to get people to listen to what you wish to say, and to look at what you want to show them. In achieving this, films play an important part in many Public Relations programmes for they can tell the public much about an organization or a product. Films can be used for training; for example, to teach young people joining a firm about the different processes they will be expected to master. They can be shown to senior forms in schools to tell school leavers of the advantages and attractions of working for a particular concern.

Other examples of the use to which films are put include 'prestige' films—documentaries with publicity for the organization cut to a discreet minimum. Special productions can be made for the information and instruction of the staff. (One leading commercial organization shows *all* its many documentaries to all its staff before general release—and they certainly appreciate the gesture)—you can use cartoons —newsreel types—travelogues—musicals—the list is endless.

Films are powerful in impact for they enable your ideas to be seen and heard at the same time, accurately and clearly. They are able to reproduce in slow motion complicated techniques, to speed up or slow down time (have you seen the film of a flower opening in a few seconds?) and enlarging to electron-microscope proportions. Films are capable of controlled distribution and of accurate assessment of impact on the audience. Another advantage is that they are semi-permanent, for a good film can last for years,

H

giving an opportunity of using some of the best brains in the country and some of the most talented people. Above all they can be a perpetual and constant evidence of sound public relations in action. All this is the potential of a few hundred feet of film.

Whatever the subject may be, there are certain basic decisions that have to be made if you are going to turn out a film which will be effective from a Public Relations point of view. The first is to have the clearest idea of exactly what it is you want to convey. What is the message, and what do you want people to know? If there is muddled thinking at the beginning, there will be muddled thinking all the way through and a muddled film at the end. It will help if you write down quite clearly exactly what the intention is, then see that it is adequately discussed by those in authority. Get an impartial opinion about it from those on whose judgement you can rely. Try and consider the project as though you were the man in the street and see if the idea itself seems to you to be reasonable and one that you could accept. Do as much research as you can into the need for a film. You may find that you write down a simple theme such as:

1. Production up—sales down.
2. Need for increased sales.
3. Present advertising campaign limited to press and television.
4. The many cinema goers—especially teenagers, not contacted through films.
5. Suitable films for this particular market with increased sales as the objective.

There is also the point that in addition to affecting the sale of the product, the image of the firm itself making the product should be enhanced. A good example of the necessity for achieving this is where you are trying to attract intelligent youngsters to join your organization or profession. Youngsters may not know enough about it, the conditions of service, the opportunities and advantages available and the best way of telling them, accurately and in an interesting manner might well be to make a film. Such a film should not only stimulate their interest but make a number of them decide that they would like to work for you. The production of such films, as with all Public Relations activity, should be intelligently and honestly done.

Having decided quite clearly what it is you want to do, the next thing to which you must give the most careful attention is deciding the audience that is going to see it. Is it going to be shown throughout the country or is it going to be shown only to the employees? Is it going to be shown for a number of years or will it be suitable for showing for a limited period of time? What age group are you aiming at? This is a vitally important question because obviously if you are going to produce a film which will appeal to the fourteen-year-old schoolboy it may have no appeal whatsoever to the adult. Is it designed for men and women or men alone? Again what kind of people? Is it aimed primarily at married women or spinsters or is it equally applicable to both? You have to have a very clear idea of your potential audience. They say that we in this country are great 'joiners' and one only has to take any town and look at the number of associations, societies, organizations and clubs of all kinds to realize how true this is. Quite a number of these bodies will offer you a ready-made audience for your film. Once you have decided that you are designing the film for a particular type of audience then do see that all the people working for you know about it and are aware of what you are trying to do and are invited to come forward with their suggestions and ideas. Particularly is this desirable with films featuring the organization. If you get thorough employee co-operation at the beginning this will ensure that later on, when you come to do some filming, perhaps in various departments, you will get a very much better job done. Also, when the film is available and being shown to the public the employees themselves will have a much greater sense of pride in the film and it will enable them to talk about it in an interesting way to their friends and relations who may, in due course, see the film. Even if you cannot consult with all the employees or indeed with a large proportion of them do see that, when the film is finished, they are given the first opportunity of seeing it. This may involve a number of showings on a shift system, but as a matter of internal Public Relations between management and employees, this is very worthwhile.

What about cost? You can make 'pilot' films yourself on 8 mm. or 16 mm. to see whether what you have in mind is 'filmable'. These can be produced quite cheaply. Equipment can be hired, and this is well worth doing under expert guidance, for such advice is easy to obtain. Magazines like *Film User* contain much useful information as to the sources from which assistance can be sought.

All Public Relations projects should be costed accurately and nowhere is this more important than in the making of a film. Films can be made on a shoe string or they can be made at an expense of thousands of pounds. They can be shot on 8- or 16-mm. cameras by one of your own employees or you can bring in a very expensive team of experts who will spend weeks in shooting the whole thing in glorious colour. You must be realistic about this and you must relate the initial outlay to the ultimate size of the audience. The purpose and ultimate audience must justify the actual expenditure. Most people are of the opinion that a second-rate film is usually not worth making at all. So if you have only a small budget it might be better to expend it in other directions. If, however, you are prepared to put up a reasonable sum, you should then end up with an absolutely first-class 20–30 minute 16/35-mm. colour film which, on free loan, will be in demand for years after it has been made because it is so good. Films which are designed for a wide audience should be the best possible that you can afford to have made.

Once you decide to make a film on a particular theme and know how much you can afford, the next job is to find a good producer. How are they to be found? Well, watch as many films as you can that have been made by other organizations. Note the names of the producers when their work is reviewed in the film journals. Study the work you like, and which appeals to you, and then meet the producer who made it. Meet two or three or even more and eventually you will have a very clear idea as to the best man for your particular film. Talk to anybody and everybody who has made films and get their collective views and experience. You may have had nothing to do with films before but if you tackle this job constructively and consistently, over a period of time you should have a good idea of who are the best producers. Nearly all film people are enthusiasts, and you will make a lot of good friends. Remember that the best films are likely to be the most expensive but probably the cheapest in the long run based on the ultimate results.

Having chosen your producer you then discuss the idea you have in mind making it quite clear exactly what you want to achieve, giving it to him (or her) in writing. The producer will then suggest that a writer should be brought in to prepare what is called the 'shooting' script. This is a most important job because the writer is really the man upon whom the ultimate success of the film depends. You can have good photography, wonderful shots of all kinds and superb acting, but nothing can affect a film more than a poorly written script. If the script is poor then your film will be worse. As writers vary a great deal, you must have a writer in whom you have complete confidence, who should be skilled at his job, intelligent and able to grasp what it is you are trying to put across and able to see the thing actually being done, visualizing it taking place on the screen. You may find that it is not possible to get any reliable estimate of what the film will cost until after the 'shooting' script is written as it is only then that the producer with his expert eye can estimate the cost of the film. In fact, you may not decide until after you have read the 'shooting' script that you are going to have a film at all. Sometimes ideas which sound very good initially and quite good in conference just don't work out when it comes to putting them into a script. You may prefer to come to an arrangement with the producer and writer that you will pay for the 'shooting' script in any event and thereafter make up your mind about proceeding with the film. When you have the 'shooting' script it will have to be considered by your board or by other people in authority in your organization. Views differ as to the best ways of doing this. Some organizations simply run off a sufficient number of copies of the 'shooting' script and distribute them to all concerned leaving them to read the script in their own way and to return it with their comments. Others prefer to arrange a script reading where the various parts are read, after careful rehearsal, to make the judging of the script as easy as possible. Sometimes the scenes are actually done 'live' so that those who have to decide can almost see the film as it will eventually appear. If this method is adopted, you will have to have first class narrators one of whom will be dealing with the story itself while another describes what is to be shown on the screen. Once you have approved the script then it is up to the producer to get on with the job and produce the best possible film. He is an expert and you must rely on his judgement but do remember that the making of a film takes quite a time.

Thought must also be given as to whether it is one film for a specific purpose or whether, in fact, it is going to be the first of a number of films. This may affect the cost, the more you make the cheaper on average they can be.

The 'shooting' of the film can be fascinating, and is a project all in the firm should welcome. Everyone from the Chairman down to the Char should be kept informed, where appropriate, and made to feel that this is 'their' film.

If filming is to be done on the company's premises it is essential that someone—armed with *complete* authority (to be used tactfully) is in control and has the power to see that the producer, director, cameramen and actors all get the support they need. You must face the fact that you are moving into an artistic world which may not be completely understood by hard-headed businessmen, but you can be quite certain your tycoons will soon spot the difference between a good film and a bad one. Anyway on general release their friends and competitors will leave them in no doubt as to the standard you have achieved.

You must realize that filming takes time. To set up the lighting alone may take some hours. Be prepared for retakes, that is where the same scene is shot over and over again.

Give all members of the staff who may be concerned ample warning so that they come prepared. Do see that those involved (which may include workers on piece-rates) do not suffer financially because of their participation. See that your electricians are alerted because lighting for filming can consume a lot of power.

The length of film shot is usually at least twice the length of that which will ultimately be shown. This is due to 're-takes' and trial shots which are experimental—and which may be quite brilliant if they come off.

The film is next cut and edited and the titles put in. The first edition is what is called the 'rough cut' and at this stage you and representatives of your firm will have an opportunity of looking at your dreams come true. They may look like a nightmare! Get the producer to run it through at least twice and on the second occasion, slowly; stopping from time to time to explain finer points of the craft.

Once the rough cut has been approved there may be a further technical stage which involves sound recording on a separate film strip and after that the combining of the picture and sound track to produce the original negative. Then comes the making of the prints. You should know roughly how many prints will be required. Factors to be considered here are whether the film is going to be handled by film libraries—including that of the Central Office of Information or distributed by you. Also the question of translation into other languages may have to be considered if overseas distribution is contemplated.

You will, no doubt, if you have a successful film made, think about making another one. The same rules apply. By all means make another one, if the means are available and film is the proper medium to put across the particular idea with which you wish to deal next. The length of a film should be only that which is necessary to achieve your object, no more and no less. It is just as well not to have preconceived ideas that you must have a twenty-minute film or a fifteen-minute film or a thirty-minute film because if the idea isn't good enough to sustain it the film will merely be dragged out to fill the footage and lose in fact as a result.

To sum up, you can tell if the film is good if it is of the right length and is one that the audience can appreciate, if it has an interesting beginning, gives a good over-all impression and is suitable to the mental age of the audience. If the film follows the best 'story pattern', and draws attention to the right facts according to their relevance and significance. If it has the maximum of movement, the minimum of dead shots, and moves at the right speed. If the music is appropriate; camera work and recording combined efficiently and naturally and if narration is involved, then this is clear, interesting and delivered at the right time. Finally if it makes the best use of all the film techniques from close-ups to cartoons. If you are surprised at the cost of a film get the producer to give you a list of the possible expenses involved, there are at least fifty distinct groups ranging from research to re-recording from set construction to specially composed music. This will help to convince your board they are getting value for money.

Pat Bowman and Nigel Ellis in their *Manual of Public Relations* (Heinemann) set out clearly the stages of production in a sponsored film. To recap what we have been considering, here it is:

1. Briefing the producer.
2. Investigation by the writer.
3. Submission of treatment and indication of price.*
4. Submission of shooting script and firm price quotation.*
5. Contract, including copyright arrangements.
6. Production conference.
7. Shooting.
8. Assembly.
9. Screening of rough-cut with commentary.*
10. Sound recording.
11. Track-laying (putting sound tracks on to fine cut print).
12. Double-Head screening (Picture on one print, sound on another).*
13. Dubbing (The Two sound tracks re-recorded into final balanced form on one complete track).

*Points at which sponsors approval is normally exercised.

14. Negative cutting, optical effects (dissolves, fades and mixes), titles, complete print.
15. Picture and sound processing on to one print.
16. Married Print.
17. Grading (of the balance of the photographic quality).
18. Show print.

Another point which deserves a careful consideration is the method of distributing films in this country.

Bowman and Ellis have much good advice on this all-important aspect of film making. For what is the use of producing a film if no one sees it? For most sponsors, non-theatrical distribution is the main outlet, and this may be to general or to specialized audiences. There are established film library organizations capable of providing a service for both home and overseas distribution and any film producer can advise on their use. The Central Film Library operated by the Central Office of Information and the commercial non-entertainment library of Sound Services Ltd. are the most effective means of circulating sponsored film in Britain. The C.O.I. can also help overseas through the British Information Services; the films acquisition department is always prepared to offer advice. Foreign government officials in London can usually give information about non-theatrical distribution facilities in their own countries.

The film libraries may be interested. Why not have a chat with the people in charge *before* you embark on film making? You may find that a few reasonable changes from your original ideas may make your project acceptable to them and thus ensure a far wider distribution than you had originally envisaged.

For a good film there is a large audience. The list of national associations is well over a thousand—(see *Whitaker's Almanack*). The 'local' list is endless. Film libraries send out *thousands of copies* of films to these organizations every year. They'll send yours if you tackle film-making intelligently and with integrity.

When distributing film direct, it is essential to have more than enough prints to meet demand and to allow ample time for dispatch and return. It is also vital to re-run prints when they come back to check that they have not suffered damage. The film libraries do this as a matter of routine.

One final tip. *Visual Education Yearbook*, published by the National Committee for audio-visual aids in Education, of 33 Queen Anne Street, London W.1, contains a wonderfully comprehensive list of indispensable names and addresses and other essential reference material.

## Filmstrips

Bowman and Ellis point out that sometimes if the money available is wholly inadequate, it is possible to produce a reasonable substitute for a film in the form of a film strip. Sometimes too the subject matter for a proposed film may on examination be better shown on filmstrip.

Not that a filmstrip should be regarded as a mere substitute; for many subjects, particularly for training use, it may be preferable to film. The lengthy holding of a single frame to show an intricate piece of machinery or a complicated flow diagram while the commentary explains it in detail is often best done by the use of film strip.

# 10 PHOTOGRAPHS

Photographs are one of the most important tools used in Public Relations. They can be used in many different types of papers, magazines, posters and also in television. A lot of people who may not bother to read even part of a paragraph will stop to look at a picture. In fact a good photograph is known by the press as 'a stopper', for it conveys the message for which it was taken. You are probably acquainted with the well known saying, 'Every picture tells a story'. A picture is what it is. A news story can be dealt with in different ways by reporters and editors, lengthened or shortened or just an extract taken from it which may alter the sense of it or lessen its impact; but with a picture it is seldom altered except possibly to be reduced in size. But, as with all other Public Relations media, it has to be the right one for the job. And the job has to be the right one for a picture. Unless you are quite certain that a picture is exactly what is wanted to carry your story, then there is no point in getting a photographer to take a number of photographs all of which will probably end up in waste paper baskets. An editor, however, is always reluctant to tear up or discard a good photograph. So whatever the Public Relations project may be, at some stage in the planning thought has to be given to the question 'Is this something which can be photographed, and ought to be photographed?' In other words, is a photograph the right way to put this particular item across to the public? Of course, everything depends upon the photographer and, as in most other walks of life there are good ones and bad ones. The best thing to do is to get to know various photographers. Go to photographic exhibitions, study their work, look at magazines and very soon you will find yourself following the work of a particular man or woman, and thereafter you may consider using them because you like their approach and have seen what they can do. Even the dullest of material can come to life in the hands of an expert photographer just as first-class opportunities can be spoiled by indifferent workmanship. pictures should be prepared bearing in mind the space that they may have to occupy in a newspaper. Very often a newspaper editor will use a small one when he hasn't got room to use a big one. After all, you can always make a small picture bigger and if you do have big pictures taken try to have them done in such a way that the main item is centrally placed or put in such a position that it can be cut down without loss of message. It is sometimes useful to be able to clip a picture to fit the size required by the editor. If your picture cannot be cut then the chances are that it may not be used at all. The size of a photograph should usually be no larger than 10 inches by 8 inches, or smaller than 5 inches by 4 inches. It is normal practice to provide whole plate ($8\frac{1}{2}$ inches by $6\frac{1}{2}$ inches) prints to the press. They should always be glossy prints, which are reproducible. A news picture should convey the message almost without using any words at all. Newspaper offices receive literally hundreds of thousands of photographs during the course of a year and, therefore, it is essential that they know, quickly and clearly, what any picture is about. Unless you are an expert, it is better to leave the actual construction and grouping of the photograph to the photographer because he will know best what is wanted and how to get it, and, in any event, if the results are not satisfactory, well then you cannot be blamed for interfering. When you send in your pictures and indeed this applies to all pictures that you have taken, they must have a caption which will tell precisely what it is about, where it was taken, the date it was taken, who is sending it in and, where people are involved, their full names and initials in order from left to right so that there will be no doubts in the editor's mind as to whom he is looking at. Caption your photograph with basic information only. If you want to elaborate do so in a covering letter or press release. If you send a photograph with a press release always *clip* your photograph to the release never pin them.

Stick the ends only of your caption either to the bottom edge of your photograph or on the back. It is necessary for the caption to be detached from the photograph at some stage prior to publication. Avoid using the reverse side of the print if you can because this can be very inconvenient for an editor who is looking at the picture and has to keep on turning it over trying to identify who the distinguished-looking man is third from the left in the back row. Don't forget that when you send in your photographs they should be sent in specially prepared cardboard-backed envelopes which prevent cracking. Put the image side towards the back of the envelope so that it won't be damaged if people write or stamp it too hard. See that it is clearly marked, telling the Post Office officials that photographs are enclosed and should not be bent.

It is sometimes important to give some indication of the size of things that are being photographed. The use of a box of matches or a coin is often very useful in doing this. It is quite astonishing, the number of misunderstandings that can arise by not indicating in the photograph the size of the object. This is particularly so when the object photographed is available to the public and may be carried (e.g. transistor radios vary greatly in size and portability) or have to fit into a small room in a flat.

As regards costs you must come to a clear understanding with the photographer as to how much you will be spending. Their charges can vary very considerably and they too will want to have a businesslike arrangement whereby you will get so many prints for so much. It pays to get a good man at his job on most occasions because there is no point in spending money on pictures that would not be accepted for publication because they are inferior. Ask the Institute of British Photographers to help you if you want a list of competent photographers. The Royal Photographic Society will also be able to assist.

There are a number of first-class photographic agencies who work closely with the press, particulars of which appear in the classified telephone directories.

Government departments, the Services, the boards of nationalized industries and a number of big commercial undertakings all have photographic libraries which may be of use to you. Make inquiries about the subjects in which you are interested.

If you have to arrange for a photographer to come into your office for work or business it is very important that he be given every possible facility. It is essential to tell all members of the staff concerned that he is coming. If he is going to photograph special types of machinery or equipment see that it is ready, properly prepared, neat, clean and tidy. Ensure that the work people who are going to operate the machinery know that they are in fact going to be photographed and do not turn up on that one morning of the week when they have forgotten to shave, or with a pair of dirty overalls or a quarter of an hour late. It must also be borne in mind that sometimes the taking of photographs can stop people working and if they are paid on a piece-work basis then this doesn't help to make things very happy in the factory or workshop. It should be clearly understood that the taking of photographs is just as much a part of the job as the actual producing of the goods being sold. Above all you do need someone in authority who can speak for top management when photographs are being taken. There is nothing worse for a skilled photographer than his coming into a workshop prepared to do a fine job only to find that he is pushed about from pillar to post, nobody can say yes or no, and he has difficulty in getting people to do what he wants in order to get the best possible photographs. The result is chaos. Some people are very touchy about being photographed at all and some organizations have an office form on which everbody who is going to be photographed gives their written consent.

There are all kinds of ways in which you may wish to consider the use of photographs. There is the straight-forward photograph of a news event, which may be anything from a celebration to a disaster. Then there are the occasions when you have to obtain special photographs of something which is being made or sold and very often great skill is required to do this to the best advantage. Then there is the imaginative, artistic shot in connection with commerce and industry. You will see samples of this kind of work in the daily press, particularly on the back page of *The Times*. Concrete towers silhouetted superbly against a setting sun —the spray from a boat being tested—you probably can recall many which have appealed to you. Start looking at your daily papers and especially the photographs they publish with a fresh eye, and you will understand why certain pictures 'made the page'. Action photographs are, usually, the work of an expert; showing a machine in opera-tion or somebody doing a particular thing which makes a good photograph. Athletics, of course, provide a splendid field for this type of photograph.

You may have wondered why so many photographs feature women and I suppose the plain truth is that as long as men are interested in women you will get pretty girls in photographs. As time goes by, however, there may be a subtle change, because the research experts tell us that the purse strings of the nation are held by women and some say no woman is ever really interested in another woman's bust, or legs for that matter. It may well be that most photographs of the future will be that of the handsome male model. A word about photographing people. You mustn't regard the taking of a photograph of, say one of your directors, or your Chairman as being a formality. There are so many different types of photographs which can be taken of individuals that this certainly is a field where there is a great deal of scope. When you look at the number of faces photographed in a hackneyed and stereotyped way looking out at you from directors' reports, financial journals, house journals and so forth, you wonder why more imagination was not exercised in photographing them to show what interesting personalities the subjects are. Most of these men hold important positions and they have mostly got where they are by character, but very, very seldom indeed is this portrayed in their photographs. If ever you are asked to arrange for a photograph to be taken of your director therefore, get the best man in the field for the job. It may well be that the last job he did was to photograph dwarfs in a circus but that doesn't matter; the thing is to get the photograph of the year of your important personality. Be bold, be resolute and, above all, be imaginative. Not all of us have got good picture sense and unless you have, leave it to the experts.

It is always wise to have, if you can, some kind of action in your picture and thereby avoid just having someone staring into the lens. This always makes a particularly uninteresting photograph and your subject usually looks stupid. However try and keep the picture simple and let it tell its own story. Don't have dark backgrounds because not only do they make a drab photograph but it is very difficult to reproduce such a photograph in a newspaper. They say English people dote on animals and babies and it is said that if you can include either, justifiably in your photograph, your picture is half-way to success. But you must keep saying to yourself 'What precisely is the object of this

I

photograph? What do I want it to say? What do I hope to achieve when it reaches the editor's desk? What do I want readers to think when they are looking at it in a house magazine or in the national newspaper or on television?' And, until you know the answers to all those questions, you cannot proceed with success. The press use a special type of paper which can be rough and it is always a good idea to tell the processer that the pictures are for press use.

Incidentally, do not forget sketches and drawings and even aerial photographs on the appropriate occasion. Sometimes a cleverly drawn diagram will tell you more than a photograph, particularly if the photograph is taken of a landscape with a mass of detail. It is much better on these occasions to have a drawing or diagram done and send a photograph of it to the editor. Also it may on occasions be worth considering taking coloured photographs. These are exciting to do and not as expensive as people think but it is very difficult to reproduce them in any number and you will probably find that the general press prefer to deal in black and white.

Whatever your organization may be, it is well for you to have a look at the photographs you already hold. Big organizations usually have a picture library. This is an extremely valuable asset provided it is well indexed and kept up to date. Often you will find the press ringing up and asking for a photograph at an hour's notice and you should, if your Public Relations are good, be able to produce exactly what they want out of your picture library without any trouble at all. If you haven't any photographs of your organization, then you might start thinking about building up a modest library, concentrating initially on annual events, leading personalities in the firm and the type of activity in which your firm engages. If you have a good stock of photographs and I mean *good* up to date photographs and not hundreds of second-rate pictures of different aspects of your firm's work, you will be surprised how often the press will be glad to have one illustrating a news point you have sent to them. Prune your library carefully from time to time remembering that some of your prints may be or may become of historic interest. It has been said that it is very difficult indeed to get any editor to print a photograph of more than eight people, unless they are cabinet ministers, because of the space required to render them recognizable and to set out who they all are. If you do have to assist the photographer in arranging a group photograph, a good tip is to concentrate on arranging the hands and feet and see that they are all doing roughly the same thing. Nothing looks worse than some with legs crossed, some with legs not crossed, arms by sides, arms folded and so forth. Don't forget that the world is shrinking. It is composed of many races, colours and religions and if you are dealing with a photograph which is likely to go overseas, bear in mind that it must not offend the beliefs and susceptibilities of those who are going to look at it: it is always worth consulting the Central Office of Information in appropriate cases.

Finally—don't overlook the law of copyright. Usually the negative will belong to the photographer unless you arrange to purchase it. If you're in doubt you are strongly advised to have a word with your solicitor. There are special forms of contract dealing with this aspect of photography.

And so once again—whether you are an industrial giant or a modest partnership there is ample scope for you in photography for Public Relations.

# 11 EXHIBITIONS

If you wish to you can study practical Public Relations all the time, and gain first-hand experience, from the receiving end. Hardly a day passes by without some form of Public Relations activity coming before you and you should be able to recognize and evaluate it. The advertisement on the hoarding or on your television set, the way a conference is organized, or a speech by your boss. All these may be part of Public Relations activity. Taking nothing for granted, look behind whatever activity interests you and try to work out why it has been done and calculate afterwards how successful it was. This you can do with certainty—so far as you yourself are concerned.

Exhibitions are a case in point. They offer excellent opportunities for good Public Relations. It is also a convenient form of Public Relations activity to study. The main purpose of participating in an exhibition is to get people to come and see what you are exhibiting. However, unless people coming to the exhibition take an interest in your stand and go away, either having seen sufficient to remember it or having been influenced enough to do what you want them to do—such as to purchase the commodity which is being displayed, it is not a success. Very few organizations in this country are big enough to stage a trade exhibition entirely on their own. Most exhibition-participation comes in the form of a number of organizations who take and rent space allotted to them on which they erect their stands.

There are, generally speaking, five different types of exhibitions:

(*a*) Vertical—This is an exhibition where the exhibits are all of one type, e.g. Motor Car Exhibition.

(*b*) Horizontal—This is the trade fair type of exhibition.

(*c*) Propaganda—This type of exhibition is used for the presentation of ideas (e.g. road safety). Careers exhibitions may come under this heading.

(*d*) 'Hotel'—These exhibitions are usually known as 'stockroom' exhibitions and are quite common. Separate rooms are booked in large hotels for different types of commodity.

(*e*) General—e.g. British Industries Fair and Ideal Home.

There are, of course, other types of exhibition which are worthy of mention although in each case they can be categorized under the above five types. The following come to mind:

(*a*) Flower shows.
(*b*) Agricultural shows.
(*c*) International exhibitions.
(*d*) Travelling exhibitions.

Organizers of exhibitions usually rent halls for a definite period, part of which is used for erecting stands. The organizer will usually provide services such as lighting, heating power, water, matting, hanging signs and features (e.g. waterfalls).

The costs of exhibiting, apart from erecting and dressing your stand, can be expensive. Sam Black in *Practical Public Relations* (Pitman) estimates that a stand in Earls Court of Olympia should work out between £4 and £8 per square foot but even this wide range will not cover all cases. To stage a 1,000-square-foot exhibit at Earls Court it is probably necessary to think in terms of a total budget of £5,000 to £7,500. These figures include everything likely to arise. They are for a single-storey stand in an existing building. If you are exhibiting overseas the cost is very much higher.

The following general programme should be borne in mind in planning exhibition policy and organization:

1. Decide to exhibit
2. Agree brief
3. Appoint designer and/or contractor
4. Approve design
5. Complete working drawings
6. Invite tenders from contractors
7. Place order for stand
8. Order special exhibits
9. Agree captions and copy and translations
10. Agree installation programme
11. Arrange services—special spare points, plumbing, etc., cleaning, phone, fire extinguishers, extra staff, security men, catering, toilets and rest rooms
12. Furniture hire
13. Flowers and plants
14. Insurance
15. Photos and Illustrations (backgrounds)
16. Copy for catalogue and leaflets
17. Order delivery of exhibits
18. Arrange staff roster, hotels and tickets
19. Order passes and badges
20. Inspection dates
21. Invitations
22. Hospitality
23. Removal plan
24. Storage of stand for future use

At any exhibition you must have been struck by the tremendous difference in appeal and attractiveness in the various exhibits. Some are much more interesting and more exciting than others. Some arouse no interest at all. Maybe they should not have exhibited at all? The first questions you have to answer when you are considering exhibiting are

'Is this the right Public Relations medium for us to employ? What do we want to do and What do we hope to achieve?' You sometimes find that it is desirable to take part in an exhibition to 'show the flag'. In other words, your competitors will have stands there and if you don't have one as well you may appear to be losing ground. This is often true of careers exhibitions organized for school-leavers, for here a most useful job of work can be done by interesting boys and girls in your organization or your firm and informing them in an interesting way about the opportunities available for them with your company.

Next time you go into an exhibition try and put yourself in the position of the person who has organized it. When you go into your local museum have a look at the way in which the exhibits are arranged, the kind of cases into which they are put, the distance between them, the lighting. Find out how far away you can read the print describing any particular exhibit, and why you went back and had a look at one a second time. You will very rapidly discover that there is a great art in putting on a first-class exhibition. Of course, when we are dealing with travelling exhibitions which are available only for a limited time, different considerations apply, particularly in the making of the stands for carrying the exhibits because often these have to be capable of very easy erection and dismantling, light in weight for easy transport from one end of the country to the other and yet strong enough to stand up to a lot of hard wear without quickly becoming dingy and dowdy. Movement can attract. So often when one is passing rows of stands, one finds that you stop automatically if something is moving. You want to see what is going on and even why it is moving. There are several advantages in exhibiting quite apart from straightforward publicity. The fact that you are there is in itself an advantage. It enables people who are directly interested in what you have to display to come along and see precisely what you have to offer and discuss your goods with people who know all about them. Next, it enables you to take advantage of an enormous 'passing trade', people who have come generally to the exhibition to see what is new. An exhibition stand, also, gives you an opportunity of distributing a fair amount of literature although you always have to be on your guard about the jackdaw-like propensities of children who will often go right through an exhibition taking every leaflet and pamphlet on which they can lay their hands and one knows that most of them will end up in the dust-bin in a matter of hours. Once the decision to take part in an exhibition has been made, the whole thing should be planned with the most meticulous detail for there are many different factors to be considered. You may even decide to run a small exhibition for the benefit of your staff. Discover the main places where people congregate, where they wait, where they have time to spend, where they have an opportunity to read and decide whether or not that place should be used for an exhibit of some kind. One of the most interesting uses I saw made of this kind of project was in connection with a big television company, who were very anxious to keep their enormous buildings spotlessly clean. They got one of their top photographers to photograph every day, one instance of a litter bug leaving rubbish without putting it into the receptacles provided. During the course of the week all these photographs formed an exhibition at the entrance to the staff canteen. They were most effective. Those who were responsible recognized the locality and very soon it was extremely difficult to find any waste paper about the place, anyway not thrown away in the proper bin! You haven't got to spend a great deal of money to do a good job at an exhibition. Some hard thinking and simple styling can often produce a stand which is the best on show because of the ingenuity and careful planning which have gone into it.

But you must have a realistic budget if you are to do the job well. To put on an ambitious first-class show can cost a fair amount of money. Exhibition designers are in great demand, particularly the more successful ones with many original ideas. If you wish to call upon their services, you must be prepared to pay comparatively high fees. If you do decide you are going to participate, don't look at it just as one more job to keep the flag flying. Don't go into it in a lukewarm manner, but do decide that you are going to do something really worthwhile and enjoy it. Don't overlook the possibility of exhibiting in conjunction with a group of traders all in the same calling, participating in an association between different kinds of exhibits which go together; such as bread rolls, sausages and mustard. You should always bear in mind that the exhibit should be one which is suitable for that particular exhibition. Curiously enough in nearly every exhibition you see one which looks so odd that you will probably wonder how in the world it ever got there. Modern materials provide wonderful scope to make attractive stands and the variety and ingenuity which goes into their construction is indeed marvellous today. So keep your eyes open and learn all the time.

The best stands are built around a straightforward idea. Don't be fussy and be quite clear and quite simple in your design. It should be well lit, no matter where it is. If people have to enter any kind of booth or stall or construction to see what is going on, then do let them be able to see clearly and without difficulty. The idea is for people to come and see what you have to show. This means traffic, and traffic must flow readily and easily. There is nothing more infuriating than to try to enter an interesting exhibit and find yourself crushed almost to suffocation point before you are able to come out again. Also remember if your exhibit is a good one it may attract queues and you must have some arrangement for dealing with this or other exhibitors may get rather annoyed. It is better to have something moving than something which makes a noise. Most exhibition organizers dislike, very much indeed, too loud a noise from an individual stand, so do not think that you will be able to attract the customers by playing a juke box or firing a toy cannon. In any event you will usually find that the contract with the organizers contain prohibitions against too noisy exhibits.

Remember that there may be people who are going elsewhere and will pass your stand *en route*. They should be able to read quite clearly what you have to say and what your exhibit is even if they are passing in a hurry. If they are able to do this, you will often find that they will come back later on to have a better look. Literature should be readily available, but not so handy that it is simply wasted by anyone who will simply stuff his pockets with it.

Most important of all, the stand should be staffed the whole time the exhibition is open to the public. Nothing is more depressing than to see quite a good stand with nobody there at all; deserted, it has a most peculiar effect, a feeling that nobody cares, not even the people who have put the stand there! Choose the staff who are going to man the stand with the utmost care. You don't need to have beautiful girls, although these can be an advantage sometimes. What is required is someone who is genuinely interested in what is going on. Someone who knows all about the product, someone who can answer the questions intelligently and in a cheerful way, even at the end of a gruelling day in hot noisy fuggy surroundings. Sometimes the effect of fine stands has been ruined simply because the people who are manning them seem to have been recruited haphazardly. Not being members of the organization exhibiting, they don't seem to have any real understanding or interest in what they are demonstrating and if they do explain, they do so in a kind of parrot fashion like a bad recording of the brief by the sponsors. Don't just put your staff there and forget about them. Theirs is a trying job, so provide them with a fair duty roster. A few personal flowers can brighten their day. If the exhibition is open until late in the evening make sure there is transport available for them to get home in a reasonable time. Don't forget to provide a visitors' book and an ideas and suggestions book. Your company will probably have decided views on the amount of private hospitality available to special visitors to the stand. If this is provided don't overdo it, or allow the staff to overdo it either. Apart from photographs for display on the stand, have the stand itself photographed. This may be of interest in the House journal if you have one, and will form part of your Public Relations archives. Keep accurate records of the number of visitors, inquiries, types of questions. Find out what interested them and why, so that you can check you are exhibiting on the right lines. Afterwards follow up all business leads the exhibition has engendered. An exhibition can be a 'snowball' P.R. exercise. There can be publicity before, during and after it. The stand and the exhibits can trigger off all sorts of other P.R. activity. Almost all Public Relations media can be used, at some time or another, in connection with an exhibition. With suitable stands you can have talks, show films and film strips, put up posters, stage special events like 'celebrity visits', distribute literature, provide material for radio and television programmes, display photographs and so forth.

Here you can combine art, science and drama to make an attractive stand which will enhance the prestige of your organization and increase its standing in the eyes of the public.

# 12 CONFERENCES

Conferences are the shop window of Public Relations activity. They are one of the best opportunities you will ever have of showing how good you are at your job. A good conference is self-evident. The very smoothness with which events are arranged and take place without any hitches or snags shows quite clearly that much time and thought has gone into the planning and execution.

Conferences can be of all kinds, the press conference lasting a short while, a morning conference with sales representatives, a day conference for staff or the annual conference of an association, lasting a week. There are national conferences, regional conferences and international conferences, and all these give an opportunity for putting into effect first class Public Relations. There are certain basic things which have to be decided as soon as you know that it is proposed to run a conference. Again you should define quite clearly what the objective is. A conference which is built around a theme always seems to go better than one involving a number of totally unrelated subjects. It is always wise to delegate the actual conference planning to a small sub-committee, and the smaller the better. Having decided to hold your conference, the next thing is to arrange a place in which it can be held. Most of the well known resorts which specialize in providing a venue for conferences are in great demand and booked up, in some cases years ahead, and so you would be well advised, if you are planning a conference, to book your conference venue as soon as possible. Once you have got your dates and your town fixed, then go there and inspect the accommodation which is offered. Never try to run a conference in a building you have not seen. Examining plans is not a satisfactory substitute for actually inspecting the rooms which are being offered to you.

You should list all the special requirements for members of your Board, staff and so on and if they are being accompanied by their wives, arrange that suitable accommodation is available for them too. In many cases you will find that there are only a limited number of rooms with baths and there may be some tactful diplomacy required to see that these are allocated to those who really should get them. Make certain that the hotel has an adequate room for a conference office and also for a press office if your conference is likely to attract the attention of reporters. Check that your business rooms are neither too big nor too small and if the business sessions are to be held in buildings outside the hotel, go and look at them too and note carefully the distance that the delegates will have to travel from the hotels in which they stay in order to attend the business sessions. Try and envisage them going under the worst possible conditions, perhaps pouring with rain and blowing half a gale and decide whether you are likely to get a reasonably good attendance at your business sessions.

Check your lighting, your heating and your acoustics in the rooms which are going to house your business sessions and consider the various ways in which the seating can be arranged. If you are going to have an exhibition of any kind, make certain that the room which is going to be provided is adequate to house the exhibits satisfactorily and that the rooms will be available in good time to set up the exhibition, before the conference actually starts. Check carefully which accommodation will be paid for by your organization and which may be given free by the hotel or the civic authorities because you are holding the conference in the

town. Check the rooms which are to be available for meetings, receptions and dances and make certain that if you are
using the same room for business sessions and social functions that sufficient time is given to clear one to allow the
other to begin. If your organization intends doing some
private entertaining see that there are sufficient rooms of
the right size available for this too. Of course a great deal
depends upon whether you as an organization are going to
be responsible for hotel accommodation or not. It is
obviously going to be very much easier to run a conference
where, apart from providing accommodation for the key
personnel concerned, the rest of the delegates make their
own arrangements. If the latter is the case, make certain
that a full list of the hotels in the town with accommodation
available and tariff is circulated to those invited to come to the
conference in good time, so that they make their private
arrangements and secure the best accommodation available.
You should check on garage and parking facilities for
delegates, also whether there is a television room, because
even during the conference some people may want to see
television, or indeed you may want to use such a room for
closed-circuit television yourself. Check also whether there
are rooms suitable for showing films and also rooms for any
of the other services which you may provide, such as
banking facilities or secretarial assistance to delegates.
Check too whether you are allowed to put up direction signs
of your own, or whether they have to conform to those
which are usually used by the hotel management. Arrange
with the hotel how the accounts are to be dealt with and to
whom bills are to be sent. Check the date and time when all
the accommodation will be available for your secretariat and
for delegates and remember to keep in close touch with the
hotel at regular intervals, telling them of the number of
delegates who are likely to be coming and also any change
in plans which you may make. You should have a completely

accurate register of all the delegates including cancellations, which should be kept up to the minute.

Having got the hotel side fairly well arranged, you should now decide on the registration fees which you think will be necessary in connection with the conference. It is always a good policy to try and make a conference self-supporting. With skilful planning this can be achieved. In deciding registration fees you must make up your mind whether you are going to charge registration fees covering the whole conference or whether you will have day to day registration fees or both. You must also decide if delegates who register on any particular day are entitled to attend the business sessions and the social functions which are arranged for that day. This is a very important point, because you may find a modest registration fee results in the delegate being given a very expensive dinner without further cost. If you have any social functions, such as coach outings or golf competitions, and the like, then you should decide whether there are going to be any additional fees, entrance fees or booking fees payable for these. Next, decide on the final dates upon which you will receive registrations and the dates after which you cannot accept cancellations and late acceptances or return money. Then, you would work out the form of registration and let your printer have the draft of this at an early date. You should also decide what will be the dress to be worn for social functions and a note of this should be included on your registration form. When you have got your form ready, you should send copies of the registration form with an outline of the programme to all the delegates and see that the conference is given the widest possible publicity in the national press, the local press, the trade press and your own house journals. In due course you should send to all delegates the final programme, with tickets for the social events, badges which they are expected to wear during the conference, cards giving details of any local

facilities which will be made available to members or delegates by the local authorities; and also car windscreen
badges if necessary. If the conference is to be attended by
wives also, remember that in most cases, double tickets will
be required.

Your organization may have permanent identification
badges which are always available, but if not there are many
types of badge which can be used. Remember, however,
that if ladies are to wear them, then pins are not always
acceptable and badges should not be too heavy or unsightly
so that they look incongruous on evening dress. There are
some excellent light-weight types of badge available and
some of them can be very attractive. You may also wish to
have them in different colours to denote officers, members
of the board, staff, overseas delegates and so on. Also do
remember to bring along a quantity of spare blank badges
and keep them at the conference office because delegates
have a habit of losing them. Request all delegates to wear
their badges (do this on your registration form and programme). If you are running a conference at which members are entitled to wear chains of office or special badges,
make certain that they are available and not left at home.

You should have a very close understanding with whoever is going to print your conference material and you
should get drafts out to your printer as early as possible—
drafts of registration forms, hotel lists to be sent out with
the invitations, the programme—including a map of the
locality in which the conference is being held (permission
for this may have to be obtained), cards which are issued by
local authorities with the amenities available in the locality,
car windscreen badges and tickets for your social functions.
You may receive again from the conference town brochures
setting out the details of the amenities of the town, you may
also want to print labels for attaching to cartons sending
out bulky programmes if they are so. So far as the badges of

the delegates are concerned, these can either be printed or typed, or of course the easiest way is to get the members themselves to write on the badges. Some excellent 'stick-on' badges are now made which adhere to any type of cloth and can be removed afterwards leaving no mark. You may also have special printing requirements in connection with any exhibitions or individual grouped activities which are being arranged at the conference.

So far as the programme is concerned, the sooner you start work on it the better. When the programme is finally put into the hand of the delegate he should be able to find without very much difficulty, what the object of the conference is, who are the important people who will be present, the names of all responsible for its organization, a list of the delegates attending, full details of business and social events with dates and times and places and dress clearly indicated. Details of where the conference office is, with times of opening and telephone numbers, details of any special identification badges, and information about any special services arranged such as banking, shorthand typists and so on. You should also give the telephone numbers of the headquarters hotels and those of key staff and a note about the town information centre, also full details of any exhibitions which are to be shown at the conference and of all sporting events which have been organized. Also the programmes should list other sporting facilities available in the area and a map of the locality. If the conference is near a weekend, details of church services should be given.

Programmes can be produced quite cheaply on a duplicator or they can be very expensive indeed if they are wirebound and produced with hard covers and glossy art paper, lavishly illustrated. This is one of the most important factors that you will have to bear in mind in financing the conference. If you are working to a set financial appropriation you will probably find that printing can run away with a very

K

substantial sum and so you should cut your coat according to your cloth. If you run a conference every year and have very much the same kind of form of programme it is a good thing to have them printed in different colours each year for easy identification. Find out also if photographs are to be used and if so, see that you have good photographs of the dignitaries who are attending. Make arrangements for the printing or duplicating of supplementary lists of delegates covering late acceptances and cancellations received after the programme is printed and circulated. See that copies of the programme are issued as soon as they are available to all the press who are likely to be concerned.

In compiling the programme, you may have to pay special attention to group activities and if you are running several functions at the same time, then see that it is clearly indicated in the programme so that members who are able to have a choice can see, preferably on the same page, what is available at the same time on any one day. Don't forget too, there must be adequate accommodation for them all to be run comfortably.

So far as the staff required for a conference are concerned it is usually better to over-staff than under-staff. You cannot always rely on the people employed by an hotel to be available at your beck and call in the running of a conference and nothing is worse than to find that a conference of some importance and size is being manned by one or two over-worked, extremely harassed, executives. Very often a conference is one of the few opportunities the staff get to meet the delegates *en masse* and establish useful and friendly contact with them. Once the number of staff to cover the conference is known, bear in mind that they too will require accommodation and that sufficient should attend to cope with the manning of the conference office, operating of any equipment, such as tape recorders, cameras and so on, and also to man any exhibitions for which the staff are directly responsible. Lay down quite clearly how and when and from where the staff are to travel and return, and don't forget to provide them also with badges. It is often a good idea to see that they are of a distinctive type or colour so that the staff can be readily identified by a delegate requiring assistance. You should also make quite clear the arrangements as to where the staff are to eat, whether they are to be treated as delegates for this purpose or whether special arrangements are to be made for them especially if manning the conference office. If senior staff are to attend the conference then they each should have a list of their duties clearly detailed so that they know precisely for what they and possibly their wives, if they are to be included, are to be responsible.

You should clear well in advance with your organizers whether a shorthand note is to be taken of any of the sessions or whether the proceedings are to be recorded on tape, or filmed or photographed in any way. You should always be quite certain that the public address system really is adequate for all purposes. There is nothing more disconcerting than to put on a panel of six or seven speakers and find that there is only one microphone on the top table which has to be passed from hand to hand.

A full list should be made of all the printed material, with spares, equipment, other materials, appliances, stationery and so on which may be required in the office. A very important point is telephones. You may want more than one and it may take a little time to get them installed. Make certain that typewriters are available, either your own or good ones from the hotel.

Check whether any stewards will be required for meetings and if so, do you provide them or are they going to be provided by an outside organization? Remember that they will require to be fully briefed as to what their duties will be, and to be provided with badges. Don't forget to prepare the signs for putting up in the headquarters hotel, and also at the places where the business sessions are to take place. You will need to obtain the necessary permission. Bouquets may be required for the ladies, if so remember to order them and watch the colours, so that they match the dress of the lady concerned—so try and get some advance information. A baby-sitting service may be considered necessary so that those who attend with young children can still come along to the various sessions and social functions and enjoy themselves. You should also request the R.A.C. and the A.A. to provide route signs to enable the delegates to reach the conference headquarters without any difficulty.

One of the things which can be overlooked is the question of transport. If your Chairman has not got his own car or the firm's car there, he may want transport laid on which is hired locally. This should be done in good time and one member of the staff made clearly responsible, being instructed quite definitely who is entitled to use it. It can be disconcerting for the Chairman of the Board to arrive at the entrance to the hotel only to find that the Deputy Chairman has borrowed the Chairman's car 'for a few moments'. Also in many conference towns, functions and sporting events are held at some distance from the conference hotels and transport is essential. To arrange adequate facilities at even a medium sized conference for V.I.P.s and special guests apart from delegates can be almost a full-time job. If you are providing tours of any kind, then you should check with the coach operators that they know exactly what is expected of them and that you are not stranded miles out with a temporary driver who really knows nothing about the place you are going to or indeed, in some cases, how to get there. Here again your transport organizer should be responsible to see that no such difficulties arise. Also, you should have a clear understanding, if it is a long coach trip, as to the stopping places and refreshments for delegates. If you are laying on coaches to travel from one place to another you must decide whether you are going to charge the delegates for travelling in it or whether you are going to provide it free. If it is free then obviously the cost must be borne in mind in working out what the registration fee is to be which is better than making a charge for using coaches.

If exhibitions are to be held either for the delegates or their ladies then you should check that the necessary bookings have been made with the exhibitors and that the necessary accommodation has been reserved at the hotel. Also ascertain whether any members of your staff are expected to man the exhibition, who is to be in charge of it and also what publicity is to be given to it, in your own printed programmes, in other printed material which you issue and in the hotel itself. Some hotels do not like to see special notices being put up by exhibitors which have not been agreed beforehand. Check precisely what are the financial arrangements in connection with the exhibition, if it is to be free or if delegates will have to pay an admission fee. Are any samples to be given away, if so, who is responsible for their safe custody? Attractive samples can disappear if left in an unattended conference office. Finally you may want to have special badges prepared for your exhibitors, and identification signs for the exhibits.

If you are going to have a distinguished speaker, remember that the best men need very long notice and they should therefore be invited as far in advance as possible. When you are sending them the invitation to speak they may know all about your organization, company or firm, on the other hand, they may not; and it is always wise to let them have as much background information as possible. You should also ask them for a photograph and biographical details about themselves and for permission to use these especially for press purposes and for inclusion in the programme. Check also if they have any objection to the press being present during their address and if they have any prepared notes which can be released to the press either immediately after the address is given or preferably before, so that it can be edited and sent out as a press release with an embargo. Check the time when they will arrive and leave, who is going to meet them, what the transport arrangements are, whether their wives are going to accompany them and who will look after them during their stay. Accommodation should be reserved for them in the principal hotel together with any special amenities such as flowers, drinks, cigarettes, cigars and stationery. You should check if their expenses are going to be met by your organization and whether they will be invited to attend all or any social functions on days on which they may be attending or throughout the conference free of charge. You should check that they have been sent a copy of the programme and an identification badge in the same way as the other delegates. You should keep your distinguished speakers fully briefed and informed of the arrangements which have been made for them and any alterations which may have to take place. You may decide that a particular member of the staff is to be asked specially to look after your distinguished speakers. Here again the bouquet question may arise. What has been said about distinguished speakers also goes very largely for official guests, but remember to check quite clearly whether all their expenses are to be met by your organization including attendance at social functions and any room service they may request from the hotel. You will find the check-list at the end of the chapter on Speeches useful in dealing with conference speakers.

Coming on to the business sessions, the most important is usually the first at the opening of the conference and you should ascertain whether the Mayor or any other local dignitary is going to welcome the delegates. You should also check whether the Chairman or whoever is going to open the conference on behalf of your organization has his address prepared in good time and if possible copies made available for release to the press in advance with an embargo. If you have local representatives in the area in which the conference is being held you may want to see that they are given special badges and have special seats reserved for them as the conference is being held on their home ground. You will need to decide if guests will be admitted to the first session only or any or all of the business sessions. If there are several sessions you may require a different chairman and if you propose having panel discussions or quizzes make sure you have a good question-master lined up. Consider whether the press are to be admitted or whether it is the intention to hold a press conference after the business sessions. You may need to make up special 'press kits' containing all the essential information each journalist will require. Check that if there is to be a break for coffee in the morning and tea in the afternoon, that there is enough room for the delegates to enjoy a cup in comfort. Ensure too that all can be served quickly. Nothing is more annoying or more likely to destroy the good atmosphere after an interesting conference session than to wait in a long queue for a cup of tea or coffee. Insist that adequate staff are made available for prompt service. Decide if they have to pay for this or if it is going to be provided free. You should check also whether there are adequate cloakroom facilities where you are holding your business sessions.

So far as the social events are concerned make sure that something is laid on for the ladies. There are endless special functions which can be put on for them; exhibitions of fabrics, perfume, china, glass, talks on travel, flower arrangement, make-up, demonstration of special cookery, the showing of films of various kinds, but do not overdo it; most wives attending want to put their feet up; they are glad to get away from domestic cares and they do not want to be over-organized. Most women are quite happy, if the weather is good, to look around the town and do some quiet shopping and relaxing. In any event whatever you decide to do, be it a simple coffee morning for the ladies, make sure that the event is properly organized and that someone is responsible for it. Regarding social activities remember to check on small details such as the booking of orchestras for dances although this is usually the responsibility of the hotel. Check your entire social programme as to the arrangements which should be made for the supply of drinks, cocktails, refreshments, cigarettes, etc., and also the dress which has to be worn on each occasion.

When it comes to dealing with such people as your Chairman, or whoever will be presiding at the conference, you will have to give great attention to detail. Most of what has been said about distinguished guests applies. Here are some of the things to be borne in mind. Book the best suite at the headquarters hotel. Will he be accompanied by his wife? Is the accommodation adequate. Does he want a private sitting-room? Will he be supplied with refreshments, his own stationery, cigarettes and so on? Have you obtained from him a photograph and biographical details for inclusion in the programme? Has transport been laid on for his use during the conference? Will his opening speech be available or anything else he may say, in advance, for release to the press? Has he been provided with full details of the programme? Will he and his wife welcome delegates at the opening reception or on any other occasion? Will they be presenting any cups or prizes to the winners of various competitions? (Incidentally, don't forget to take the cups and prizes with you.) Will they be holding any private parties, and if so, who are to be the guests? Are you to be responsible for seeing that they are marshalled and arrive at the right place at the right time? Are special invitations to be issued? Will there be dinner parties or cocktail parties? If so, remember such things as place cards, table plants, flowers, cigarettes, cigars, microphones. Will the wife of the Chairman be doing anything specially for the ladies who will be accompanying the delegates (such as a coffee morning)? Finally will he be wearing any special badge? (If so don't forget to take it with you.)

If your Vice-Chairman or Vice-President is to attend, then you should make arrangements for some of the duties to be carried out by the Chairman and some by the Vice-Chairman and their wives likewise. This sometimes calls for diplomatic and tactful handling, but all these details should be worked out well in advance so that both parties know precisely what their duties are to be. Consideration must also be given to the menus for special luncheons, dinners, and so on. You will sometimes find that your Chairman or his wife have very strong views about this and this also is a matter which should be given consideration in good time. If cocktail parties are given, it is always wise to indicate quite clearly when they will start and when they will finish; and do see that they finish reasonably near the time stated as they can become very protracted and consequently rather more costly than you planned. If you hold dinners with speeches, make certain that you have a toastmaster ready if it is the custom to do this. At receptions and dances make certain that there is a table available for your Chairman and his party, which is large enough to accommodate the guests who will always want to come along and meet him and have a chat. See that a waiter is assigned specially to look after that table and that there is an adequate supply of refreshments. Make certain that those who are to be invited to share the Chairman's table are notified of the fact.

Where you are running a conference in conjunction with local branches or societies, then you should make quite clear what the functions of the local people are; whether they are going to be on the top table and share the running of the conference with your Chairman or whether they will play quite a subsidiary part. If the former, you should have early consultations with them about local arrangements, particularly such things as sporting facilities and so on. If visits are to be paid to local works or societies make certain that all the arrangements are organized well in advance and that when the delegates go, there is a senior delegate who will assume responsibility for the party and who will say a few words of thanks after the visit or the hospitality. You should also find out whether any other local dignitaries are to be invited to business sessions or social functions.

A conference in itself is not news. They are being held throughout the country every week. It is unusual for a statement which is made at a domestic conference to hit the headlines, but nevertheless, wherever possible the press should be given facilities for covering the conference and accordingly you should check that adequate press releases have been sent out at appropriate intervals giving the press details of the conference organization. Copies of the full programme should be sent as soon as they are available to all the press that are likely to be interested. You should indicate quite clearly when setting out the programme which sessions are to be opened to the press and don't forget to send programmes to the agencies, to the B.B.C. and I.T.N. As I have said before, you should also clear with your speakers whether they have any objection to the press being present and if so, whether they would be prepared to meet the press afterwards. You should also clear this with any V.I.P.s or local dignitaries who may be attending. Check also whether the social functions are to be opened to the press. Ascertain if a press office is required and, if there is to be a press conference at the end of each day's business, make certain that there is a suitable room available with seats, tables, and facilities for providing some refreshments.

Decide who is to conduct it and see that there are adequate telephone facilities available. Ensure that they have a list of delegates with some information, if it is wanted, about the more interesting personalities attending and see finally that one member of the staff regards it as his principal duty and is in charge of co-operating with the press.

When the conference is over as soon as it can conveniently be arranged, you should hold a post-mortem with all the staff concerned in the organization to see what went right, and even more what went wrong, so that your plans for next year can ensure an even better conference. Letters of thanks should be sent as quickly as possible to all those who have in any way assisted in helping to make the conference what it was. Accounts should be settled promptly. A report should be made on the conference organization and running to those to whom it should be given. The transcripts of the speeches which have actually been given, should be submitted to those who made them before publication and finally, if the conference produces the right kind of material then it should be printed and made available for those members of your organization who were unable to attend. Then get down to some hard work so that when the next conference is held the members can see that some real progress has been made in the past year.

# 13 PUBLIC RELATIONS IDEAS AND ACTION

What kind of person are you? You may think you are efficient, capable, hard-working, and ambitious. What do people think of your firm? You might have an idea of the views some customers, employees or suppliers hold. You and your organization deal with many people; many various sections of the public. The sum total of all these opinions is your reputation; and your reputation is crucial to the success of your business. If they trust and respect you, and like your product and service, they will deal with you. If they don't, they won't.

So if you have a fine product—give an excellent service —people will do business with you—*provided they know about you*. A business must be efficient to survive, but nowadays it must also be seen to be efficient. Not just to customers, employees and shareholders, but to the man in the street. Every business is part of the community and you and your firm are becoming more and more interdependent with those around you. Public Relations is not something you can make up your mind to do or not as you please. Public Relations is something you have, whether you want it or not. Peter Drucker in *Managing for Results* (Heinemann) says that there are three different dimensions to the economic task: (1) the present business must be made effective; (2) its potential must be identified and realized; (3) it must be made into a different business for a different future. Each task requires a distinct approach. Each asks different questions. Each comes out with different conclusions. Yet they are inseparable. All three have to be done at the same time: today. The future is not going to be made tomorrow. In all this Public Relations plays a significant part.

Public Relations is not an end in itself. It is a means to an end. Eric Webster in his two quite remarkable books no firm should be without, *How to Win the Business Battle* and *How to Get the Better of Business* (John Murray) points out that one of the great disadvantages is that we appear to speak the same language. If you ask an employee to bring you a cup of tea you know from experience that he is unlikely to present you with a brick. This sort of thing lulls you into a sense of false security. You draft a simple instruction to switch the tea break from 3.30 to 3.45 and labour relations go up in flames. Why? People are emotional. People take things personally. People see things and words and actions from entirely different points of view. The thing that matters about words isn't what they *mean*. It's what all the others *think* they mean. The first essential of good P.R. is the ability to communicate clearly. When a manager says something is 'for the good of the company' he may mean it. When a man says 'for the good of the firm' he means for *his* good. The manager may see the organization as a collection of machinery and people intended to produce a profit for the shareholders. The employee clearly sees that the whole concern exists to provide a job for *him*. Good P.R. is essential if this cleavage of opinion is to be bridged and both employer and employee made to realize that ultimately their interests are identical.

You are in business to make a profit, but the community is taking an increasing interest in how you make it and what you do with it when you have made it. Commerce and industry today have a social responsibility to discharge, undreamt of in the days of *laissez-faire*. Each businessman must decide what his policy is going to be about relations with local Chambers of Commerce and trade organizations —about activities taking place in the community both where he and his employees reside and where they carry on business—about the opportunities given to employees for education and getting on. Incidentally, who gets the credit for new good ideas in your organization ? Public Relations in action has many facets—relations with employees—and employee organizations such as trade unions—with suppliers—customers—consumers—shareholders—the community—Government departments and the vast range of 'influence formers' such as the press—radio and television —and important sectors of the public such as teachers, the professions, etc.

In dealing with employee relations you should examine and compare your wages structure and policy with that of similar organizations bearing in mind changes in the cost of living—technical developments and local conditions. Even although there may be a clearly laid down procedure for dealing with these problems with the trade unions concerned nevertheless the *manner* in which discussions are instigated and conducted can be all important to the eventual outcome. Management seldom loses by taking the employees into their confidence. Their failure to do so is often disastrous. A wise company keeps employees informed of company problems. Have you given adequate attention to pension schemes, retirements, possible redundancy and the ways of making this as limited as possible in its inevitable effect ? What about amenities, conditions of work and safety and efficiency ? In so many companies all these things *are* studied most carefully by experts who in due course submit their reports to top management where decisions are taken approving the recommendations made, and that's that. A new rule is introduced, a new system of work. Seldom are those most immediately concerned told *why* and their whole-hearted co-operation invited in making the innovation a success.

Have you given adequate consideration to recreational

facilities for employees? preferably *with* your employees either on a company or community basis, even if you can't afford to provide expensive private sportsgrounds you may encourage and support an office netball team to play in the local park. To what extent are the families of employees encouraged to take an interest in the activities of your organization? A harmonious office atmosphere can be engendered if new members of the staff on being confirmed in his or her appointment are invited to bring their parents in on a visit to see where they work and meet other members of the staff. Subsequently when parents and children talk about work they both know who and what they are talking about and a better understanding makes for a better relationship with the firm and enhances its reputation. It would pay some firms with a rapid turnover of junior staff to have a 'parents advisory committee' to point the way to better relations.

Every employee has at some time or other personal problems—often of an intimate nature. You must decide the extent to which your organization can or ought to provide assistance and guidance. Once the policy has been settled and suitably qualified staff made available all employees should be informed clearly but tactfully of the service afforded. A room where confidential matters can be discussed in private, in the firm's time if this is reasonable, temporary financial assistance on a limited scale—advice on where, when and how the social services operate and their help can be obtained. All these are things which go a long way to build up sound employer–employee relations. Nowadays something much more helpful is required than a staff outing and a Christmas party.

During the war, factories were visited by airmen who flew the aircraft made in them. The effect on the workers' morale was very great. No longer were they doing a monotonous job which would have a part in shaping an end product they hardly ever saw and with no 'human factor'. They had now met the man who flew the machine and pressed the particular button they made. It transformed the whole attitude and atmosphere. Does something similar happen at your plant or factory?

What do you do if you have a labour dispute? You should have an adequate and honest Public Relations plan prepared for use in such a situation if you are so unfortunate as to be involved. Remember that if a company is silent during a labour dispute the inference which will be drawn, rightly or wrongly is that the company policy is too biased to be brought out into the open. Why not anticipate and have a clear understanding with labour leaders of the steps to be taken *promptly* in the event of a dispute so that it can be settled around a conference table. Does anyone ever really benefit in the long run from a strike? Have you ever done any research into your 'labour relations', even to the limited extent of asking those who have been with you some time why they like working for you and those who leave after a short period why they are going?

The Marathon Oil Company of Ohio U.S.A. have one of the best public relations programmes in the United States, and issue a wonderfully comprehensive manual of P.R. to company managers. One section deals with company policy in an emergency. Here is the check-list. Who does what in an emergency? Who notifies Fire and Police Departments? Who notifies Company management? What action do employees in the affected area take, and to whom do they report? What action is taken by employees in other areas? Who notifies the Public Relations Division? Who notifies the local press? Who acts as the official spokesman for the company? What action, if any, is taken to reassure employees in other areas? What action if any, is taken to reassure employees' families? Who is responsible for these actions? Are dealers and suppliers notified, and if so, who notifies them? Who has developed information on safety records and safety programmes, both company-wide and for this installation? Who has this information in immediately usable form? Who is responsible for gathering detailed facts on the event? Who prepares an official summary of the incident? Who initiates an investigation? This really is the art of administration by the use of anticipation. If you want to check how good your own P.R. is, see what 'disaster plans' are in being in your organization.

In considering Public Relations activity in connection with manufacturing or trading activities each department should be made aware of the value of adequate and effective Public Relations. How? If you haven't a Public Relations department or consultant, get someone who is an expert to come and give your departmental heads a talk on the subject. The Institute of Public Relations runs a speakers' panel which may help.

Each department has its own particular functions, needs and problems. Those dealing with sales and advertising, who have an expert knowledge of the needs of customers and consumers, markets and marketing, are in a strong position both to apply public relations intelligently and effectively and to assist other departments with their experience and information.

There is here, however, one matter which should be firmly grasped by top management. Is the Public Relations activity of the organization to form part of or an adjunct to advertising and/or sales, or is Public Relations to be a function of the whole of top management—as it should be? Expert advice should be sought on this problem if Public Relations is to be introduced into an existing organization with the goodwill, advice and support of all associated with the concern. The advertising and sales departments can often render signal service in the fields of research.

Never lose sight of the fact that Public Relations is the

L

deliberate, planned and sustained effort to establish and maintain mutual understanding between an organization and its public. This can in practice affect everything from the design of work overalls to the method of setting out the figures in the company report.

To do effective Public Relations for traders you must know the trade, its history, its trends and its operators. The first class Public Relations officer studies his subject as a whole and should be as well and even, perhaps, better informed about much of the organization's activities than the majority of other employees. Often by this knowledge Public Relations can assist sales promotion to become more effective. The dividing line between the two in this kind of operation can be a very fine one indeed.

Good Public Relations is not based solely on a knowledge of your own organization. It is founded on accurate and up-to-date information about all who serve and supply you. They too have their own problems, and enlightened action on your part can often help to solve them. The crucial point of Public Relations is in its effect on dealings with the consumer or customer. If it fails here it may well nullify all the good work done by all the other departments put together.

You can never have too much up-to-date information based on sound research. After all, the satisfied customer is one of the main objects of business. Look at all your activities in this connection with a fresh eye—a Public Relations eye—has your notepaper moved with the times?—is the room where callers wait for you pleasant and attractive? —have you rung your office recently and got first class service from the switchboard when they *didn't* recognize your voice?—are demands for the payment of overdue accounts framed in the most effective way?—to ensure quick payment and renewed custom—are complaints promptly and satisfactorily dealt with? collated and considered to avoid repetition?—are customers encouraged to look behind the scenes—dare you let them? Have you ever asked customers for ideas? Try it one day, you'll be surprised, possibly quite pleasantly. Have you really got an intelligent policy about Christmas gifts to customers, or are you torn between indiscriminate generosity and fear of a parsimonious reputation?

All these are matters upon which skilled public relations guidance can be obtained.

What part do you—your organization and its employees—play in the community? Often the reputation of a concern depends more on what its members do outside working hours than in. You may be making a product with a limited market which does not include 'the man in the street'—and yet it is his daughter whom you hope will answer your advertisement for secretarial staff. How do you stand in their esteem? Management should have a detailed plan which should provide for establishing and maintaining deserved local support.

Public Relations plans dealing with the relations between a company and its shareholders offer one of the most interesting and challenging opportunities available to any firm. Do they take an interest in you, apart from a financial one? How much do you tell them and how? Are your company reports easily read and understood? To what extent has their format changed over the last ten years? Are shareholders ever invited to visit the plant on 'open days'? You may one day need fresh capital and those already holding shares in your company may be your best source. Will they support you? They won't, you know, if you treat them merely as numbers in the register of shareholders.

Think about all these problems—get expert advice where necessary and put to top management sound plans setting out the ways in which you think Public Relations can help to answer these questions and achieve the overriding objective—say, the continued wellbeing of the company.

Much of the foregoing may not be applicable to every organization and may well be beyond the capacity of the staff you now employ—but it gives some indication of what Public Relations in action means. It is intended to start you thinking along Public Relations lines. If you have well-organized and efficient Public Relations it can help in recruiting staff, and keeping them, making them proud to belong to your organization, it can help sales promotion, and enhance the reputation of your concern in the community.

What does this cost and how can you tell if you have had value for money ? Face the fact at once that you get from Public Relations what you are prepared to put into it and quality, which has to be paid for, always tells. Also it will be extremely difficult for you ever to evaluate completely from an accountancy point what precisely has been the result of a particular Public Relations campaign. It is like throwing a stone into a pond—the ripples continue over a wide surface long after the initial impact.

The manner in which the action is organized will of course vary according to your needs. A leading American company has a member of its board who is responsible for (1) Personnel; (2) Employment practices; (3) Management development; (4) Executive supervision of public relations policy; (5) Special assignments in the broad field of human relations.

In an enlightened company Public Relations is understood and applied by *all* members of the Board. It is a good idea to begin with to assign this function to one member of the Board who has the capacity, interest and energy to do a sound job and ultimately to educate the other members of the Board.

You may decide to publish a statement of your policy and aims. Many American companies have done so, notably

Marathon Oil, Ford, Du Pont, Armour, Swift and Company, the General Electric Company and a host of others. The statements cover everything from the adopting of a high standard of business ethics to patriotism, and many are well worth considering. Most of these companies will send you a copy of their Public Relations policy on request.

If you are embarking as a member of top management in industry into Public Relations the following will be of special interest to you.

Speaking before the Institute of Industrial Relations in America, James W. Irwin, then with the Monsanto Chemical Company of St. Louis, Missouri, offered these suggestions to businessmen in connection with the qualifications for a Public Relations administrator for an industrial enterprise:

1. See that you as the chief executive of your corporation select qualified executives for your Public Relations posts. Take them into your full confidence. Give them enough authority that, using their experience and judgement, they can overrule your operating executives in matters of public and industrial relations. In overruling such executives, they should of course, stand on their own feet and if they guess wrong too often, they should be thrown out just as you would do to any operating executive to whom you have always given autonomous authority within his field.

2. Give them authority to study and overhaul your policies and activities, so that you will always be on the right or ethical side of any argument and I don't necessarily mean only legally right. I mean morally and humanely right.

3. See that your labour relations man takes your Public Relations man into full confidence. If your Public Relations man doesn't sit in on discussions of labour policies

and in labour negotiations, he should be nearby and he should have access to minutes, files, daily discussion. He should be treated as a member of the organization and not as a fireman who goes out blindly trying to put out a fire without proper background or the vital information he needs in his contacts.

4. Use third party pleading in management–labour relations. This means an informed Public Relations man steadily contacting influential people. Unless your Public Relations executive has rank high enough to be respected, he cannot contact the people who will be most valuable to you and your company.

5. Be sure that a trained newspaperman—a newspaper editor preferably and a man who has been grounded in the fundamentals of labour relations—heads your plant publications.

Unless he has this training, he will be scared to the bone by the mistakes he will make, and he will cost you money and wasteful hours, as well as many heartaches in your relations with your employees.

6. Think fast and act first in getting the company side to the public, press and radio first in any labour disputes, even to the extent of announcing a strike and scooping an international labour representative. And when it is settled let the company announce the terms and resumption of operations instead of letting the announcement come from the union office.

7. You—the chief executive of your corporation—must hold press conferences for newspaper and radio men if labour difficulties, if indictments, if any other serious developments break. Make yourself available for questions and all cards-on-the-table interviews. Forget that you have home obligations or that you have a date at the club. Make yourself available at the convenience of the newspaper and radio men. They are your sole contacts

with your employees and your public in any kind of dispute. Whether it be with labour, the Government or a competitor!

(*The Dartnell Public Relations Handbook*, 1961)

Although you may not agree with all the foregoing there is much sound common sense in the suggestions made.

Once you have decided to embark on Public Relations and evolved a policy and formulated a plan constant checks are necessary to see that it is carried through. Public Relations needs a 'progress chart' just as much, if not more so, than any normal manufacturing operation. A full annual report on Public Relations activity is an essential part of the audit of any organization's work. And the yearly review should extend not only to projects actually carried out but also to the policies underlying them.

As *Dartnell* says 'Good Public Relations *must* stem from sound and progressive *thinking* on the part of top management. Some people like to believe and like to have others believe, that their principal function is to tell top management how to think and act. They make a grave mistake, because the top men in a corporation, an association or a mercantile establishment cannot delegate their thinking or the responsibility for their thinking or their actions to anyone. What they can delegate, as *Fortune Magazine* once pointed out, is a considerable part of the responsibility for the explanation of the actions and thinking of the corporation.'

The main job of Public Relations is to communicate—not to manage. There are many ways in which you can put your Public Relations thinking to work.

Settle your policy—prepare a plan—and tell all concerned what you propose to do and how you are going to do it. This includes employees, customers and shareholders. See that someone in authority directs operations. Inform

those who work for you of the significance of your organization to the community—invite your employees' friends and
relations to visit your concern—remember the human side
and publicize worthwhile happenings to employees whether
they are directly concerned with their work or not. If you
have something worth seeing—arrange for those who can
benefit to see it—youth employment officers—teachers—
senior school pupils—and groups in the community where
opinion matters. Consider what you do and can do for the
children of employees apart from the usual idea of a
Christmas party—encourage all concerned with your organization to play a full part in the community—be generous
with time off, if they are doing a praiseworthy job. Meet the
press—and see that your senior executives do too. Arrange
some kind of get-together with representatives and top
management at least once a year. Check the telephone
manners and letter-writing style of all concerned periodi-
cally. If these are not up to standard arrange ways of
improvement tactfully and in a way which ensures they
understand its importance. Welcome new customers with
a special letter—devise a means of keeping in touch with
satisfied customers—they can be your very best advertisement. It is wise to have an intelligent policy in dealing with
competitors, and to support to the fullest possible extent the
activities of your trade associations. It will help you to see
that complaints are dealt with promptly by someone who
has the power to do something about them quickly if they
are justified. You would be well advised to give serious
thought to the methods by which complaints from members
of your staff are at present dealt with and ensure that
adequate time is given by senior executives to what, although
it may be unpleasant, is a very necessary part of the
machinery of harmonious employment. You might like to
consider the giving of a reward for good ideas—promptly
and with publicity, whether they come from inside the firm

or without. See that the history of your organization is written by someone who can write a history—year by year —in an authoritative and interesting way. See that those who can speak do speak about your organization whenever suitable opportunities present themselves or can be created. Don't take customers for granted—appreciate them. The list of activities is endless. Use your imagination.

What about 'special events'?

If you've got something to show—show it. Factory— workshop—plant—installations—getting people to have a look at it can do a lot of good—employees' families—the press—sections of the public who may be interested— facility visits—or open house are special events which can pay excellent Public Relations dividends. First decide what you want to achieve, ascertain precisely what is the object of the exercise? Next decide who's going to be responsible for the visit. Prepare with care your list of guests—very often a good mix of suppliers and customers blend on a visit very happily, then decide on the date of the visit with one eye on any special date or anniversary of significance to your organization to give the visit greater interest and impact. How much are you prepared to spend on it? The facilities you will have to provide for a well-organized special event such as an open house are very similar to those required for a conference—although of course as a rule they are required for a much shorter space of time.

Check parking reception, children, cleanliness, registrations, sign posting, staff instructions, refreshments, badges, speeches, etc., publicity, in just the same way.

The Marathon Oil Company gives the following list:

## Ideas for Special Events

*Open Houses*

1. Anniversary of completion of first well in field.

2. Anniversary of opening of refinery, or purchase by company.
3. Anniversary of opening of pipeline or pump station.
4. General company anniversaries.
5. Industry Events.
6. Completion of new facilities, new offices.
7. Purchase of facilities, or entry into new community.
8. Significant achievements, new production records, important safety records, etc.
9. Opening of a new design service station.
10. Announcement of new process or new product.
11. Community events, local salutes to industry, historical commemorations, Business–Education Day, etc.

### Dedications, Celebrations and Similar Ceremonies

1. Dedication of new facilities.
2. Dedication of new equipment, office buildings.
3. Dedication of new parks, recreation areas, etc.
4. Dedication of historical markers or commemorative plaques.
5. Ground breakings, layings of corner stones, etc.
6. First barrel or first can produced.

### Tours

1. In connection with other events, such as students during Public School Week, professional societies during National Engineers Week, etc.
2. By press, in connection with any newsworthy announcement.
3. By retired employees, an annual event.
4. By college classes, as recruiting or customer development programme.
5. Publicise regular visitation day, for instance, 2 p.m. on each Thursday, when guides will be available to conduct tours for anyone who appears.

*Other Events*
1. Banquets, dinners, luncheons to which local opinion leaders are invited.
2. Annual reunion of retired employees.
3. Presentation of scholarships, awards, etc.

Public Relations in action can be of great benefit on many occasions. As has been explained, the public really consists of many sections of the public and each presents its own problems. Sit down and list some of those with whom your organization is from time to time concerned, shareholders, government departments, the voluntary organizations in the community, the trade press, competitors, customers overseas. How much do you really know about what they think about you and your organization?

Given ideal circumstances what would you like them to think about you? Where do you fall short in deserving this opinion? What can you do to put matters right—'to improve the product'—and consequently the image, deservedly? If you are prepared to start thinking about these matters from a Public Relations point of view you are more than halfway to finding the proper solution. For the same basic principles apply in each case.

But satisfactory results don't just happen. They have to be earned. They are usually the product of a deliberate, planned and sustained effort to establish and maintain mutual understanding between an organization and its public.

For that *is* Public Relations.

# 14 THE INSTITUTE OF PUBLIC RELATIONS

## The Institute—What it is and What it does

### HISTORY

The Institute of Public Relations is the only organization in the United Kingdom devoted exclusively to the study and development of public relations. It was founded in 1948 by a group of public relations officers from commerce, industry, central and local government, all of whom felt the need for an organization to represent the rapidly expanding profession in which they were engaged.

The Institute has since firmly established itself and now has nearly three thousand members.

At the beginning of 1964, the Institute became a body corporate and in doing so achieved official recognition of itself as the professional body representing organized public relations practice. The Constitution adopted at that time contains, as appendices, a code of conduct and the machinery necessary to apply it.

### DEFINITION AND MEDIA OF PUBLIC RELATIONS

The Institute defines public relation practice as 'the deliberate, planned and sustained effort to establish and maintain mutual understanding between an organization and its public'. This definition implies a two-way flow of information, the public relations officer providing the necessary channel. Advertising and isolated publicity campaigns do not in themselves constitute public relations operations, although they may be part of them.

The media of public relations include the written and spoken word, broadcasting and television, films, exhibitions and other visual aids. The aim of the public relations practitioner, whether he is an employed public relations officer or a public relations consultant is, in short, to establish and maintain a relationship of maximum understanding between his firm or client and those sections of the public with which his organization is concerned.

'Public Relations Officer' (P.R.O.) is the most widely accepted title for public relations practitioners, but a number of other titles are also used.

## OBJECTS

The Institute's main objects are:

(a) To promote the development of public relations for the benefit of the practice in commerce; industry; central and local government; nationalized undertakings; professional, trade and voluntary organizations and all practitioners and others concerned in or with public relations.

(b) To encourage and foster the observance of high professional standards by its members and to establish and prescribe such standards.

(c) To arrange meetings, discussions, conferences, etc., on matters of common interest, and generally to act as a clearing house for the exchange of ideas on the practice of public relations.

### THE PUBLIC RELATIONS OF PUBLIC RELATIONS

The Institute is concerned with the provision of information to the general public, and to specialized groups, about the practice of public relations in order to correct the many popular misconceptions which exist and to present a fuller picture of the work of public relations practitioners.

The Institute is also concerned with such matters as professional standards, ethical issues and codes of practice.

Close relationships are maintained with the Press, radio

and television through the Institute's secretariat. There is a speakers' panel whose members are available to speak on various subjects connected with the practice of public relations.

## MEMBERSHIP

The categories of membership within the Institute are:

Honorary Life Members, Fellows, Members, Associates, Retired Members, Overseas Associates, Affiliates and Student Members.

*Honorary Life Members* are individuals, from within or without the Institute, on whom the Council are empowered to confer this honour in recognition of outstanding services.

*Fellows* are Members on whom the Council have, by secret ballot, conferred Fellowships 'in recognition of distinguished public relations work'. Fellows are entitled to use the suffix 'FIPR'.

*Members.* Membership of the Institute shall be open to:

(*a*) Individuals who at the date of their application are 28 years of age or more and whose applications are acceptable to the Council providing that they have had at least five years' comprehensive experience in and that they are qualified to undertake the practice of public relations as defined in Clause 3 of the Memorandum of Association.

(*b*) Individuals who at the date of their application are 28 years of age or more and whose applications are acceptable to the Council providing that they have had at least two years' comprehensive experience in and that they are qualified to undertake the practice of public relations as defined in Clause 3 of the Memorandum of Association and providing further they shall have previously been awarded the Institute's Diploma in Public Relations or (prior to 1972) that they shall have passed the Institute's Final Examination.

Members shall be entitled to a Membership Certificate, to exercise full voting rights in the affairs of the Institute and shall be entitled to use the letters 'MIPR'.

*Associates.* Associate membership shall be open to individuals normally resident in the United Kingdom who at the date of their application are twenty-one years of age or more and whose applications are accepted by the Council provided that either:

(*a*) they shall at the time of their application have been professionally engaged in public relations practice for a minimum period of three years, OR

(*b*) they shall at the time of their application have been so engaged for a minimum period of two years and shall have passed the CAM Certificate in Public Relations or (prior to 1971) the Institute's Intermediate Examination.

Such persons shall be entitled to use the description 'Associate of the Institute of Public Relations' and to exercise full voting rights in the affairs of the Institute.

*Retired membership.* Retired membership shall be open to any Fellows, Members or Associates who have retired from active business life and whose applications are acceptable to the Council. Such persons shall retain the right to use any letters or descriptions to which they were entitled at the time of their applications, be entitled to receive the monthly and annual publications of the Institute and shall be entitled to receive notice of and attend but not vote at any general meeting of the Institute. In the event of a Retired Member subsequently resuming full-time employment he shall revert to his previous class of membership and shall pay the appropriate annual subscription from 1 July following the date of resumption of such employment.

*Overseas Associate.* Overseas Associate membership shall be open to individuals normally resident outside the United Kingdom who would qualify for Associate membership were they living within the United Kingdom and whose applications are acceptable to the Council. Such persons shall be entitled to use the description 'Overseas Associates of the (British) Institute of Public Relations' but shall not be entitled to exercise voting rights.

*Affiliates* are persons, normally resident in the United Kingdom, who are engaged in public relations work but are not yet eligible for associate membership or who are associated with or interested in the practice of public relations. Affiliates may use neither suffix nor description and are not entitled to vote in the affairs of the Institute.

*Student membership.* Student membership shall be open to individuals who at the time of application are taking or proposing to take a course of education or training leading to the IPR Course Certificate or undertaking examinations for the CAM Certificate in Public Relations and whose applications are acceptable to the Council. Such persons shall not be entitled to put any letters or descriptions after their names or to receive notice of or attend or vote at any general meeting of the Institute.

A Student Member shall only be entitled to retain such membership until he shall have passed all parts of the CAM Certificate or until 30 June following the date of three years of Student membership whichever period is the lesser provided that at its discretion the Council may extend the latter period in respect of any individual. In determining the three-year period of Student membership of any individual the Council shall take into account any previous period or periods of Student membership he may have had.

All applications for membership must be made on a form available from the Institute and must be endorsed by two sponsors already in membership of the Institute. Each application is considered in detail by the Membership Committee who then make a recommendation to the Council upon whom the final decision rests. The Membership Committee may call for additional information or may require the applicant to appear before them for interview in order to satisfy themselves that the highest standards are maintained in all categories.

## MEETINGS AND EVENTS

One of the most valuable functions of the Institute is to provide opportunities for the exchange of information and active co-operation amongst its members.

In addition to the tuitional courses, the Institute arranges evening discussions, debates, film shows, facility visits, one-day and weekend conferences—all designed to increase members' knowledge of the theory and practice of public relations.

Luncheon meetings are held from September until June to which are invited distinguished guest speakers from industry, government, the professions, etc. A general meeting is held annually.

## PUBLICATIONS

The Institute publishes a monthly magazine 'Public Relations'—the only publication of its kind in this country devoted solely to this subject. Articles of general and educational interest on subjects connected with public relations are published in this magazine, the centre pages of which carry information about Institute activities. The Institute publishes occasional papers as supplements which, like 'Public Relations', are sent to all members.

## GROUPS

The Institute's Constitution provides for both professional and regional groups. At present there are groups for members who are local government public relations officers and those in voluntary movements and for those working in the

M

Midlands, East Midlands, East Anglia, North-East, North-West, West of England, Wessex, Scotland and South Wales.

## ADMINISTRATION

The Institute is governed by a council which is elected by the voting members—Honorary Life Members, Fellows, Members and Associates—all of whom are eligible for nomination to the Council.

The Council elects a Board of Management and various committees—Professional Practices, Disciplinary, Membership, Education, Public Relations and Development. In addition, special sub-committees and panels are appointed, as necessary, to discuss matters of common interest with other organizations.

## LIBRARY

A number of books on public relations and allied subjects are available for reference by members in the Camden Public Library.

## REGISTER OF MEMBERS

The Institute maintains a register of all Honorary Life Members, Fellows, Members, Associates, Affiliates and Overseas Associates. This is published annually.

## BRITISH UNITED PROVIDENT ASSOCIATION

The Institute has a group within the British United Provident Association which entitles members of the group to a 10 per cent reduction in their subscription to the B.U.P.A. Any person who is an individual subscriber to B.U.P.A. can, upon joining the Institute, transfer to the Institute's group thereby securing the reduction in subscription. Full details of the group are sent to all persons upon admission to the Institute. The administration of the I.P.R. group within B.U.P.A. is the responsibility of Group Management Ltd, Prama House, 267 Banbury Road, Summertown, Oxford.

### ANNUAL SUBSCRIPTIONS AND ENTRANCE FEE

The annual subscription (inclusive of 'Public Relations'), payable in advance on 1 July of each year, is

|  | £ | s. | d. |
|---|---|---|---|
| Fellow | 12 | 12 | 0 |
| Members | 10 | 10 | 0 |
| Associates | 8 | 8 | 0 |
| Retired Members | 1 | 1 | 0 |
| Affiliates | 6 | 6 | 0 |
| Associates and Affiliates under 25 years of age when subscriptions are due | 4 | 4 | 0 |
| Overseas Associates | 8 | 0 | 0 |
| Student Members | 2 | 2 | 0 |

> ('*Public Relations*' *is not inclusive but available at a reduced annual subscription of* £1 1s. 0d.)

Persons applying for admission, and subsequently elected, pay an entrance fee of £5 5s. 0d., except in cases of persons under 25 years of age when the application is made, when the entrance fee is £1 1s. 0d. Student Members pay no entrance fee until transfer to another category.

Those members elected during January, February and March pay half a year's subscription for the period to the end of June; members elected during April, May and June pay a full year's subscription which carries them to 30 June in the following year. Subscriptions are payable by bankers' order.

### INCOME TAX RELIEF

The Institute is recognized as a professional organization by the Commissioners of Inland Revenue. This means that under Section 16 of the 1958 Finance Act, those members paying income tax under Schedule E can claim tax relief on their subscription.

### FURTHER INFORMATION

Further information may be obtained from the Institute of Public Relations.

## Public Relations Consultants Association Ltd.

### AIMS AND OBJECTS OF THE ASSOCIATION

1. The Public Relations Consultants Association has been formed with the object of promoting the interests of Public Relations Consultancy by providing members with the opportunity for consultation and co-operation and of providing facilities for Government, public bodies, associations representing industry and trade and others to confer with Public Relations Consultants as a body and ascertain their collective views.

2. A Public Relations Consultancy is defined as a firm qualified to advise on public relations and to implement that advice where public relations techniques are recommended or which provides a specialized service and is able to recommend a comprehensive range of other services.

3. One of the primary objects of the Association is to ensure that Public Relations Consultants shall be qualified to advise on public relations matters and shall act for the clients in a fiduciary and professional capacity.

4. The Association supports the Institute of Public Relations. The Association is a trade association with corporate members, while the Institute is the professional body with individuals as members.

5. The Association is a medium through which its members can consult with each other on matters of trade and professional interest, and affords a forum through which consultancy practice may be co-ordinated.

6. Matters are constantly arising in which it is an advantage to Public Relations Consultants to obtain the opinion of their colleagues in the profession. The Association will keep in touch with matters which affect consultancies and will put its advice and assistance at the disposal of members in any matters of difficulty arising in the course of their practice.

7. The Association is also a medium through which the public can be informed as to the standing, experience and qualifications of its members.

8. The Association intends to draw up a Code of Consultancy Practice with the object of defining the qualifications and obligations of a Public Relations Consultancy and its relations with its clients and of setting up an accepted standard of professional practice.

9. The Association will help to promote confidence in public relations consultancy and consequently in public relations as a whole.

10. Only Full Members of the Association are entitled to vote.

11. Subscriptions are to be based on an annual fee income, this figure to be taken to the last audited account or to the 1st January prior to application.

| ANNUAL FEE INCOME | ANNUAL SUBSCRIPTION |
|---|---|
| Over £150,000 | £400 |
| £100,000—£150,000 | £300 |
| £50,000—£100,000 | £200 |
| Under £50,000 | £100 |
| Under £25,000 | £50 |

### WHAT THE PUBLIC RELATIONS CONSULTANTS ASSOCIATION OFFERS TO MEMBERS

The Public Relations Consultants Association is a trade Association devoted to promoting the interests of consultancies, improving practice and disseminating its code of practice (see below) as widely as possible. Members receive the benefits of joint negotiating strength, common standards and policies, a forum to exchange ideas and experience, a common meeting ground with other professional bodies in allied fields.

The secretariat will provide an information service, in addition to carrying out its administrative functions.

In addition to these general benefits, the following are some of the projects which will be tackled by the P.R.C.A. during its formative years to the advantage of its members.

### 1. *Consultancy Register*

An annual register of members will be issued with frequent updatings. This register will give the following information on its members:

Name; address; telephone number; names of directors; staff size and expertise; a summary of services offered; information on clients (discretionary).

The register will be issued free to all P.R.C.A. members and a comprehensive mailing list will ensure wide distribution.

Through its independent secretariat, the Association handles requests for information about its members on a strictly impartial basis.

### 2. *Public Relations Programme*

Consultants need organized public relations for themselves. The Association is instigating an active programme of promotion giving information on as wide a scale as possible on the scope of services offered by consultancies. This will be invaluable in creating a greater knowledge and understanding by management of the value of P.R. consultancy services.

### 3. *Management Services*

Consultancies face ever increasing operating costs. The needs of clients for extra services and specialized skills have to be met, in many cases with no increase in the rates of fees. Without skilful management profit margins shrink. With this in mind the P.R.C.A. will develop management aids to assist members. The secretariat will be able to draw on considerable experience and expertise from within the membership and its professional advisers. It will assist managements with problems in complete confidence.

### 3(a). *Analysis of Consultancy Costs*

One of the first tasks of the P.R.C.A. will be to assemble an analysis of representative consultancy costs and income, similar to the I.P.A. Annual Analysis of Agency Costs. Each year members will be invited to report their results on a strictly confidential basis for impartial analysis by categories of cost and income.

### 3(b). *Analysis of Staff Salaries*

The P.R.C.A. aims to fill another gap in the knowledge required by P.R. consultancies, by producing an analysis of salaries paid to staff of all levels.

### 3(c). *Financial Management Practice*

A manual of financial management practice for P.R. consultancies is contemplated giving an outline of the type of systems and procedures necessary for the sound financial and accounting management of consultancy. Subjects will include: forecasts; costs and profitability; financial accounting; budgets; and similar aspects.

## 3(d). *Staff Administration*

The P.R.C.A. will study the staff policies of members to include current practice on working hours, pension schemes, holidays, sick pay, bonuses and other benefits. This information will be useful to members requiring guidance on their own arrangements.

## 4. *Consultancy/Client Relationships*

A consultancy and a client may disagree about the consultancy's terms of business and their respective rights and responsibilities. Often disputes could be avoided if their business relationship had been stated clearly in an agreement. The Public Relations Consultants Association will set out some suggested provisions for use in client agreements and will aim to arbitrate if required. The Association's code of practice will be available as an additional guideline.

## 5. *Members' Activities*

As a trade body, the P.R.C.A. will promote the interests of Public Relations Consultancy by providing members with the opportunity for consultation and co-operation and the Association will hold meetings, conferences and seminars when appropriate.

## 6. *Library Services*

The Association will seek to build up a collection of case histories and like material; it will also aim to act as a repository for archive material which will be available for study by members.

## MEMBERSHIP CRITERIA

Each application will be examined by the Membership Committee of the Association. A ballot for admission will be held at a meeting of the Association's Board of Management. The decision of the Board is final, and it is not obliged to give any reasons.

A. *How to apply:* Application forms are obtainable from the Association. Additional information may be requested subsequently by the Membership Committee.

B. *Business Location:* Consultancies whose main place of business is in the United Kingdom or the Republic of Ireland.

C. *Nature of Services:* The applicant must be able to supply a full range of services to clients, or if it is a specialized consultancy, be in a position to recommend a full range of other services. The Association welcomes both small and large consultancies into membership.

D. *Clients:* The applicant consultancy must provide, not necessarily for publication, a list of its major clients and the length of time each account has been held.

E. *Professional Qualifications:* At least 75 per cent of the applicant consultancy's directors or partners must have a minimum of 5 years' public relations experience.

F. *Experience:* The applicant consultancy must have been operating as a public relations consultancy long enough to have demonstrated its experience and its financial stability.

G. *Independence:* The applicant consultancy must act independently in professional matters, not being controlled by any client whose public relations it handles, or by organizations engaged in the sale of media.

H. *Financial References:* The applicant must provide financial referees: i.e. its banker and accountants and/or auditors. This information will be held in complete confidence by the Association's accountants.

I. *Standards of Practice:* The applicant consultancy must undertake to observe the Association's code of practice, bye-laws, rules and constitution. (See below.)

J. *References from Members:* The applicant must supply the names of two members of the Association as referees regarding its professional standards of practice.

### CODE OF CONSULTANCY SERVICE

A Public Relations Consultancy is defined as a firm qualified to advise on public relations and to implement that advice where public relations techniques are recommended or which provides a specialized service and is able to recommend a comprehensive range of other services.

1. A member firm has a general duty of fair dealing towards its clients, past and present, fellow members and the public.

2. A member firm shall not engage in any practice which tends to corrupt the integrity of channels of public communication or legislation.

3. A member firm shall not intentionally disseminate false or misleading information and is under obligation to use ordinary care to avoid dissemination of false or misleading information.

4. A member firm shall not purport to serve some announced cause while actually serving an undisclosed special or private interest.

5. A member firm shall safeguard the confidences of both present and former clients and shall not disclose or use these confidences to the disadvantage or prejudice of such clients or to the financial advantage of the member firm.

6. A member firm shall only represent conflicting or competing interests with the consent of all those concerned.

7. A member firm shall not, without the client's consent, accept fees, commissions or other valuable consideration

from anyone other than the client, in connection with services for that client.

8. A member firm shall inform a client of any shareholding or financial interest held by that firm in any company, firm or person whose services it recommends.

9. A member firm shall not propose to prospective clients that fees or other compensations be contingent on the achievement of certain results, nor shall it enter into any fee agreement to the same effect.

10. A member firm shall not submit to a potential client detailed proposals for a public relations campaign or programme before appointment by that client without payment of a reasonable fee. This does not preclude a member firm from giving information about the services it can provide, its suitability for the assignment, or the general approach it would recommend.

*Note:* When in any doubt as to the application of this code, please apply for guidance to the Association's Consultancy Practices Committee.

## International Public Relations Association

The only international public relations organization in the world, its members often cooperate on international P.R. programmes. It consists of individual members, not firms.

## C.E.R.P.

Centre Européen des Relations Publique. The European Centre of Public Relations. It acts as a platform where public relations people from European countries can discuss their profession. It is a grouping of national bodies, formed in 1959. Its aims are carried out by three working parties, CEDAN, CEDET and CEDAP:

CEDAN is the European Conference of National Public Relations Associations, and is in charge of the co-ordination of the activities of the national bodies to reach agreement on professional principles, ethics, and practice.

CEDET is the European Study Group for Public Relations and Communications Techniques, and is a forum for the exchange of views between specialists who practise in various professions but are all interested in humanistic studies and information.

CEDAP is the European Committee for the Application and Development of Public Relations, and is composed exclusively of professionals in public relations in a personal capacity; senior advisers, directors, associates of public relations agencies.

Information about CERP and its working parties is available from the General Secretary, M. Alfred de la Motte, 10 Quai Paul Doumier, 92 Courbevoie, France.

## Public Relations Societies Abroad

The Institute of Public Relations has recognised Societies in Argentina, Australia, Belgium, Brazil, Canada, Chile, China, Denmark, Finland, France, Germany, Greece, India, Ireland, Israel, Italy, Japan, Mexico, Netherlands, New Zealand, Norway, Philippines, Rhodesia, Spain, South Africa, Sweden, Switzerland and the United States of America. Addresses may be obtained from the Institute.

# 15 EDUCATION FOR PUBLIC RELATIONS IN THE SEVENTIES

A new three-way education system for public relations came into effect on 1st January, 1970. It combines maximum flexibility of choice and opportunity with the higher educational standard called for by the Board of Trade in connection with the Institute's official status as a recognized professional body.

From the beginning of 1970 students and members have the following options:

1. The I.P.R. Course Certificate.
2. The Higher National Certificate in Business Studies (P.R. Option).
3. The Diploma in Public Relations.

The new Diploma supersedes the old Intermediate/ Finals system of examinations and, with the academic year 1969–70 well under way, no further *new* student registrations for the Intermediate are being accepted.

To avoid inconvenience to students already in the pipeline, the phase-out period for the old Intermediate/ Finals extends to Spring 1972.

There will be examinations for the Intermediate in 1970—Winter, as usual.

There will be examinations for the Finals in Spring 1971 and Spring 1972.

People now studying for the Intermediate should continue their courses, as usual, and should proceed to the Finals in the normal way.

Candidates for the Finals who have sat papers but have

not completed the examination by 1st September, 1972 (i.e. by the beginning of the academic year 1972–73) may request the Institute for a transfer to the new Diploma system.

Taking the three options in turn—

## The I.P.R. Course Certificate

This course has been available since September 1966. It was designed specifically for people who wish to learn basic public relations principles and techniques. It is, essentially, a nuts and bolts course and has proved useful, popular and successful over the last three years. It has been incorporated, without change, in the Institute's new education system.

The course lasts one year and consists of one evening lecture per week together with one practical workshop per week. The examination consists of two three-hour papers taken in a single day, normally in late May or early June. Papers are marked in London by an independent panel of examiners and results are usually known within five or six weeks.

To take the course a candidate must first register as a student member with the Institute. He must have a minimum educational qualification of four 'O' level subjects in the General Certificate of Education, one of which must be English language or literature, or he must have passed another examination acceptable to the I.P.R. Council as being of an equivalent standard.

There are no lower or upper age limits and candidates need not be employed in public relations. Candidates are, however, expected to be intelligently aware of the environments in which public relations must work and to have a general knowledge of the institutions and organizations likely to be relevant to this work. Particular emphasis is placed throughout the course on command of English and the examiners are required by the Institute to look for evidence of a candidate's ability to express himself clearly in good standard English.

The International Correspondence Schools offer a course in preparation for the examination. For obvious reasons, the I.C.S. course cannot include the practical workshop sessions.

## The Higher National Certificate in Business Studies (P.R. Option)

In July 1968 the Department of Education and Science informed colleges of further education that it had approved the Public Relations syllabus, prepared by the Institute, for inclusion as a second-year vocational subject in the day-release courses leading to Higher National Certificates in Business Studies.

The Public Relations syllabus bears the Department's code number 'H 22' and Business Studies students wishing to avail themselves of this new vocation educational opportunity are advised to make enquiries at their local colleges of further education. Because the H.N.C. is part of the national further education system students are not required to register with the Institute. However, registration as a student with the Institute is not expensive and it offers certain benefits, details of which may be obtained from the Institute's Secretariat.

In common with many other professional bodies, the Institute of Public Relations accepts H.N.C. examinations as qualifying students for exemptions on a subject for subject basis in its own professional examinations. The Department of Education and Science's obligatory subjects in every H.N.C. programme of studies are Applied Economics I and II (H 1 and H 2). There are around twenty other subjects in the H.N.C. total range and of these there are three which carry exemption from the I.P.R's Diploma examinations, the H 22 making the fourth:

H 10  Business Organization;
H 13  Sociology of Industry and Commerce;
H 20  Marketing;
H 22  Public Relations.

Because H 22 is only now moving into the H.N.C. system, not all colleges yet include it in their courses. Where a student is faced with this situation he should get in touch promptly with the Institute to discuss possible solutions: for example, one alternative would be to consider the I.P.R. Certificate as a substitute for H 22, while another would be to postpone studying the 'P.R. subject' until, the H.N.C. completed, the student proceeds to the Diploma in Public Relations with three of his subjects, as shown above, qualifying him for exemption. In any case the Institute will always be glad to advise Business Studies students.

The H.N.C. is a two year course, recognized by Industrial Training Boards; age and educational qualifications are laid down by the Department of Education and Science and are set out in college prospectuses. Both the courses and the examinations are handled by the education authorities.

## The Diploma in Public Relations

The curriculum for the new Diploma in Public Relations is more broadly based than the curriculum for the Intermediate/Finals. It takes into account the trends in public relations that have become apparent since the Institute set up that system in 1956. Among the more noteworthy trends are the rate of establishment of public relations departments within industry, the development of financial public relations, the rapid expansion of public relations in Local Government and the steadily rising stature of public relations as a senior management function.

The Diploma is, therefore, designed to meet the needs of the Nineteen Seventies and to provide a recognized professional qualification such as may be earned in other business spheres.

It consists of two Parts: Part (which shall be known as the C.A.M. Certificate in Public Relations) is at the standard of the old Finals and consists of six Papers—

Part I 'A'
  1 Public Relations;
  2 Business Organization;
  3 Marketing;

Part I 'B'
  4 Media—P.R. Serviced (i.e. editorially controlled);
  5 Media—P.R. Directed;
  6 Human Relations in Industry and Commerce;

The Institute regards a four-year span as a reasonable time for Diploma candidates to complete Part I, bearing in mind that all candidates will be working full time in public relations and be subject to customary work pressures. Within this time span candidates may proceed at their own pace with the proviso that Papers 4 and 5 should be taken together. Part I 'A' must be completed before Part I 'B' is commenced.

Exemption on Paper 1 (Public Relations) will be available to holders of the Intermediate (Associate) examination certificate and the I.P.R. Course Certificate provided that the candidate achieved a pass mark of 70% and fulfils all other eligibility requirements (see pp 180-1).

Part II. A thesis. An interview/discussion.

Candidates may propose their own thesis subject which must be some aspect of communication within the context of public relations. They should obtain the Institute's ap-

N

proval in writing of the proposed subject before beginning the study.

A thesis may be submitted at a time mutually convenient to the candidate and the Institute and agreed, in advance, in writing.

A candidate must attach a Declaration of Sole Authorship to the thesis and the Assessors will be required to look for evidence of sound knowledge of the subject and original thinking.

The Institute will hope to publish successful theses, format and style still to be decided, but copyright will remain with the candidate.

The interview/discussion will follow as soon as may be mutually convenient to the candidate and the Institute after the thesis has been accepted by the Assessors.

Members of the Institute who have already passed the Finals examination may now proceed, without delay, to Part II of the new Diploma. Successful completion of Part II will enable the member to place 'Dip. P.R.' after his name.

[During 1967 and early 1968, when the desirability of a Diploma in Public Relations was first discussed, it was thought that M.I.P.R's by examination would become entitled to place 'Dip. P.R.' after their names as soon as the first Diploma had been awarded. During the development of the Diploma curriculum, with Part I of the Diploma being at the standard of the old Finals, it became apparent that this would create an unacceptable discrepancy.]

## Eligibility Requirements

The Institute has laid down that candidates for the new Diploma in Public Relations should normally possess:

(i)   At least one approval 'A' level or the equivalent; or
(ii)  At least 5 'O' levels (including English) or the equivalent and be at least 18 years old.

Exceptionally students may be accepted who are at least 19

years old and who have had at least three years' relevant business experience.

All students should normally be employed in the field of communication, advertising or marketing but exceptionally other students may be accepted who can satisfy the college concerned of ability to profit by the course and to complete it satisfactorily.

All students must be registered with CAM.

## Application for Membership

Application for membership of the Institute will continue to be made in the usual way. Application forms are available on request from the General Secretary. The category of membership that may be accorded an applicant—Affiliate, Overseas Associate, Associate, Member—will continue to be a matter for the Membership Committee which will, as hitherto, make its recommendations to the Council. By ruling of the Board of Trade in connection with the Institute's professional status, full Membership cannot be accorded to any person under 28.

## Diploma Courses and Examinations

Courses and examinations for Part I, and arrangements for the availability of these courses, will be handled by 'C.A.M.'. C.A.M. will also nominate one of the Assessors for Part II. Candidates for the Diploma will be required to register with C.A.M.

## The C.A.M. Foundation

C.A.M. is 'The Communication, Advertising and Marketing Education Foundation'. It is a company limited by guarantee, not having a share capital, and registered with the Charity Commissioners as an educational trust.

The founding members—known as the Constituent

Organizations—are, at present, The Institute of Public Relations, The Advertising Association, The Incorporated Advertising Managers' Association, The Incorporated Society of British Advertisers and The Institute of Practitioners in Advertising, while the Institute of Marketing will also be represented on the Board of Governors.

The Foundation was established, primarily, to 'promote . . . the general advancement of communication, advertising and marketing education at all levels . . . to provide educational facilities, both general and specialized, for persons taking part in or intending to take part in the communication, advertising and marketing processes . . . encourage and provide liaison between state-operated education . . . and to assist in the improvement of educational and training standards . . .'

The I.P.R. gladly accepted the invitation to become a founding member of a project that was not only very much in line with the Institute's own thinking but held promise of valuable streamlining of overlapping educational activities combined with greater influence in regard to the organization of courses, particularly in centres outside the London area. The I.P.R., which has played a full part in the development of the Foundation during 1969, will have two nominees on the Board of Governors (eleven members) and, by function, the General Secretary of the Institute will be an ex-officio Governor.

The Director of C.A.M., Mr. John Dodge, takes up the appointment of Director of the Foundation early in November. He was the unanimous choice of the Selection Panel (seven members) on which the I.P.R. was represented.

Mr. Dodge, who is a Cambridge graduate, comes to the Foundation from the National Council for the Training of Journalists where he has been Director for the last eight years. He served on the Editorial Board of the Thomson Foundation and on the Board of the U.N.E.S.C.O. Mass

Communications Centre at Strasbourg. With George Viner, he edited the standard textbook 'The Practice of Journalism'. Mr. Dodge began his career in journalism with the Northamptonshire Evening Telegraph and later was a reporter and sub-editor at Reuters.

The Foundation is expected to be in action early in 1970 and it is thought that the Director will have made the course arrangements required to permit the first C.A.M. examinations to take place in 1971.

It is proposed that candidates for the Diploma in Public Relations will be awarded the C.A.M. Certificate upon successful completion of Part I. It is hoped that this will entitle them to put 'P.R. C.A.M.' after their names, to be replaced by 'Dip. P.R.' when Part II has been successfully completed. The C.A.M. Certificate will be a meaningful qualification in its own right.

The Institute has prepared the syllabus for each Paper in Part I. These will be handed over to the Foundation shortly. In the meantime, copies of all syllabi are available from the I.P.R. Secretariat.

# 16 EXAMINATION QUESTIONS AND DIPLOMA SYLLABUS

## Certificate Examination—29 May 1969

### Paper I—Three Hours

*Candidates are reminded that particular emphasis is placed on clarity of thought and expression.*

### ANSWER FIVE QUESTIONS ONLY
### ALL QUESTIONS CARRY EQUAL MARKS

1. I.P.R. Code of Professional Conduct: Clause 10:
'A member shall not propose to a prospective client or employer that his fee or other compensation be contingent on the achievement of certain results; nor shall he enter into any fee agreement to the same effect.'
What is your interpretation of this clause?

2. James Young, reporting the I.P.R.'s 1969 Annual Conference in 'Campaign', said: 'The P.R. man is paid to represent his cause in the most favourable light.' Do you accept this as a correct interpretation of the role of public relations, and give your reasons.

3. Many P.R. departments of advertising agencies have been converted into subsidiary companies with names quite different from those of the parent companies. Why do you think this has taken place?

4. Describe the main responsibilities of a staff P.R.O. in a large industrial company. What advantages and disadvantages has he over a P.R. consultant serving such a company?

5. Your company has produced a 20-minute 16-mm. colour film to explain the correct way to use a new product. You may choose any product or invent one. Draw up a brief plan for the distribution and showing of the film. How can the C.O.I. be of any assistance?

6. The Government has been criticized for having too many P.R.O.'s (Information Officers), and the Opposition has sought to gain public support by promising to reduce their number if returned to power. How are P.R.O.'s used in the Government service, and what would be the likely effect of reducing their number?

7. What is the Central Office of Information? How can its various departments be of assistance to the exporter?

8. (A) If a consultant engages a photographer to take pictures for a client's house magazine, which the consultant is producing, who owns the copyright of these pictures, the photographer, the consultant or the client?

(B) Why, when submitting photographs to the press, is it essential to be sure that your organization or client owns the copyright, and to make this clear on the backs of all prints?

(C) If you wished to reproduce a newspaper cartoon in your house magazine what would you do regarding the copyright of the cartoon?

(D) What is the position regarding copyright if you wished to quote a scene from Shakespeare or a passage from Dickens in your house journal?

## Certificate Examination—29 May 1969

## Paper II—Three Hours

*Candidates are reminded that particular emphasis is placed on clarity of thought and expression.*

### ALL QUESTIONS CARRY EQUAL MARKS
*Candidates must answer ONE of the following two questions.*

1. You are the P.R.O. of a firm which manufactures electronic equipment at a factory in the south-east. Owing to your firm's success in exporting, it wants to expand its output. It cannot get permission to extend its existing factory and has decided to open a second plant on a trading estate in the north-east. List the various publics likely to be affected by this decision; and, in each case, indicate *briefly* what needs to be explained to them, and the methods you would use.

2. You are the public relations adviser to a national society, supported by voluntary funds, which exists to protect wildlife in Britain. The society has plans for a substantial expansion in its work, but needs a much greater annual income to achieve its purpose. You have been asked to suggest a P.R. plan of action to raise these funds.

Outline the steps you would advise—indicating briefly v hat they would involve.

### *Answer FOUR of the following six questions*

3. What is meant by the minutes of a meeting? In what respect do minutes differ from an agenda? Taking any topic you wish, draft a specimen minute and re-write it as a newspaper item.

4. Discuss the advantages and disadvantages of flapped captions, fixed captions, and direct captions on pictures circulated to the press.

5. Name three major printing processes and describe their characteristics.

6. Explain briefly any *SIX* of the following terms:

| | |
|---|---|
| Blueprint | Imprint |
| Centre Spread | Leak |
| Deckle | Mock-up |
| En | Photo-montage |
| Facility visit | Protocol |
| Film Strip | Slug |

7. What are the purposes of an external house journal?

8. A public relations practitioner is often required to be responsible for some or all aspects of a special event. Give up to five examples of the form such events may take and list the main items that should be considered in their planning and administration.

## Associate Examination—4 and 5 June 1969

### Paper I—Three Hours

*Principles and Practice of Public Relations*

*Candidates* must attempt questions 1 and 2 *and* any three *others*

1. What points would you make if you were asked to give a talk about public relations to a meeting of a trade association? None of the members would know much about the subject, and you have to be fairly general in your approach. Would you use any visual aids?

2. You live in a pleasant, tree-lined road which is under threat of being widened and hence having all the trees felled. This would completely alter the character of the road. A Protection Association has been formed to fight the decision of the local authority's Highways Committee. What publics do you have to reach to try and get the proposal altered?

3. How would you go about convincing a sceptical client of the professional basis of your work. What particular points from the I.P.R. Code of Professional Conduct would you use as illustrations?

4. You are advising an industrial company which has suffered from several well publicized changes of top management and consequent reorganization. Morale is low at all levels. A new chief executive has been appointed and he wants a P.R. programme outlined which will help restore confidence in the company both internally and externally.
Produce a brief which explains what kinds of activity might help achieve this aim.

5. How could research help you in measuring the effectiveness of a public relations campaign of your own choice?

6. A dish washer manufacturer finds that one of the components in a new model has been faulty, causing the machine to fail after about a month's use, thus resulting in a fall in sales. What P.R. steps would you advise to meet this situation?

7. How could a staff P.R. man be aided by using the services of a consultancy?

8. One of the Sunday Colour Magazines has a splendid story in it about your company's centenary. What use could you make of this feature?

## Associate Examination—4 and 5 June 1969

### Paper II—Three Hours

*Press Relations*

*Candidates* **must attempt questions 1 and 2** *and* **any three** *others*

(The term 'Press' includes sound radio, T.V. and newsreel films, etc., throughout the whole of this paper.)

1. The Chairman of a large British motor manufacturing company, of which you are the Chief P.R.O., is shortly returning to London from a world tour by air during which he has obtained substantial export orders for the firm. He has cabled you to say that he wishes to announce his success to the Press immediately he is back in London.

Outline the plans you would make to obtain the publicity he seeks.

2. You are the P.R.O. of a steamship company which, in 3 months' time, is to introduce a new ship for tourist cruises in the Mediterranean and the Caribbean. The liner has attractive and novel amenities for 1,000 passengers all accommodated in one class, a good range of entertainments on board and a first-rate cuisine.

Write a news story, in not more than 250 words, announcing the introduction of the ship (using your imagination in describing the novel amenities) and produce it in a form that should be generally acceptable to the Press without any alteration.

3. You are an Account Executive in a P.R. consultancy and you have been assigned the task of preparing a Press editorial campaign for a new client who makes exclusive pottery. The client's firm is not well-known but its products

are good and it is anxious to develop a home and export market. You are not concerned with its advertising programme.

Outline the recommendations you would make to the head of the consultancy on the way the campaign should be carried out.

4. An old-established firm of British tea importers reaches its 200th anniversary in six months' time. Your P.R. consultancy has been commissioned by the company to plan celebrations aimed to publicise the event in the Press as widely as possible.

What would you consider to be the most effective proposals you could submit to the firm?

5. The charitable animal welfare organization of which you have just been appointed the staff P.R.O. is failing to attract new members and is losing existing ones. The governing body believe that to a great extent this is because of a lack of Press and other publicity for the excellent work the organization does in informing the public on the way to take proper care of domestic animals.

How would you aim to improve the Press publicity?

6. The Chairman of the company for which you have been invited to be the P.R. consultant has told you that he will judge your competence by the volume of Press editorial space you obtain for the firm.

Would you accept a commission from the company if this were to be a condition of your contract, in the hope that you could produce the publicity the Chairman wants; or would you decline an offer made with such a stipulation? Give your reasons for whichever choice you would make.

7. You have become the P.R.O. of an undertaking which manufactures furniture and has suffered loss of orders because of indifferent workmanship. It has now changed some

of its staff and has recruited first-rate craftsmen with the result that its products are as good as those of any of its competitors. There is still no recovery of business, however.

How would you try, by a Press editorial campaign, to restore the reputation and prosperity of the company? What media would you use and why?

8. The Managing Director of the firm in which you are the Chief P.R.O. is a difficult man who is constantly telling you how to deal with the Press. His ideas are usually impracticable. Although the situation is becoming intolerable and you are contemplating resignation, you are well experienced in P.R. and decide that you will make a final effort to persuade him not only that you know your job but are convinced that you can do it to his satisfaction if he will leave you to do it in your own way.

What would you say to him?

## Associate Examination—4 and 5 June 1969

## Paper III—Three Hours

*Printed material, house journals, advertising*

*Candidates must answer* **four** *questions:* **Question 1** *and* **One Question** *from* **each** *of Sections A, B and C.*

*Question 1 carries 40 marks; the other three questions carry 20 marks each.*

1. (**Compulsory**)

(*a*) You are the P.R.O. of a manufacturing company which, along with all other companies in the field, has unfortunately suffered a drop in sales over the past year.

   At a Board Meeting the Accountant has suggested, as a solution to the consequent drop in profits, that the Company restrict its advertising, cut down on printed material, and cease publication of the House Journal.

   As P.R.O., you are responsible for these three activities. What points would you include in your reply to the Board, to justify expenditure in these three directions?

(*b*) After listening to your reply and to those of other sectional heads, the Board of Directors decides on a reduction of 15 per cent in your annual budget. What action would you take to cope with the new situation?

*Section A     Printed Material     Answer* **one** *question only*

2. A junior colleague has been present during a meeting with your printer and asks you to explain the following terms he had overheard:

| | |
|---|---|
| (*a*) Web Offset | (*f*) Em's |
| (*b*) Sans type | (*g*) Half-tone |

(c) Lower case    (h) Imitation Art
(d) Rule          (i) Linotype
(e) Points        (j) Bleed

3. You have been asked to address your fellow students on a weekend course, on the subject of 'What the P.R.O. should know about Print'.

Outline the points you would make in a 20-minute talk.

*Section B      House Journals      Answer* **one** *question only*

4. As newly-appointed Editor of your Company's long-established quarterly external House Journal, primarily for customers and potential customers, you have become concerned at the increased cost due to rising circulation, which has mounted steadily for the five years before your appointment.

You wish to establish that this growth in circulation has been accompanied by increased readership. Accordingly, your most recent issue included a tear-out reply-paid card which readers were requested to return if they wished to remain on the mailing list.

The number of reply-cards received six weeks after publication amounted to 10 per cent of circulation. What action would you take?

5. The manufacturer of a grocery product with a very high frequency of repeat purchase is anxious that his field Sales Force should feel that the Company is backing their sales efforts.

There is a monthly meeting in each of the eight regional Sales Offices, and an Annual Sales Conference for all representatives. The Company already publishes a general staff magazine, but the Managing Director now seeks your views on the contribution that a special publication for the Sales Force could make to maintain and improve Sales Force morale.

Prepare a brief report for your Managing Director, setting out the possible role of such a journal, with recommendations regarding format, content and frequency of publication.

*Section C*          *Advertising*          *Answer* **one** *question only*

6. What separate roles do the following people play in planning and executing an advertising campaign:

(*a*)  The Advertising Manager;

(*b*)  The Account Executive;

(*c*)  The Advertisement Manager.

7. Concern has been expressed by one of your Directors that much of the money spent on the Company's advertising is wasted. As the executive responsible, what practical steps would you take to eliminate any such waste in your own Company?

How would you reassure him that this, in your opinion, is not true?

## Associate Examination—4 and 5 June 1969

### Paper IV—Three Hours

*Exhibitions, photography, films, audio-visual aids*

**Please** *read the questions carefully*

*Candidates are required to* **answer question 1, either** *question 2* **or** *3, and* **any** *three other questions.*

**All** *questions carry the same marks*

1. Explain the main work of a Press Officer acting for a national trade exhibition open for two weeks in London. (Complete your answer in not more than 300 words.)

2. You are the Public Relations Officer of a Trade Association concerned with the building industry and it has never previously made a film. Your Publicity Committee asks you to advise for or against the value of making a film to recruit more members for the Association. Presume the total amount of money available for making a film is £3,500.

Outline your recommendations to the Publicity Committee.

3. You are the P.R.O. of a firm taking part in an important national exhibition in London. Your company has booked space and signed the contract for it. Your Chairman says to you, 'The Board want you to be entirely responsible for this whole job up to the time of opening. Then the Marketing Director will take over and he will be responsible for all staff on the stand. But you will be responsible for clearing up.'

List, step by step, with some indication of time, what you would expect to do to complete this instruction.

(Do not concern yourself with budgetary matters.)

*Answer any Three of the following questions*

4. You are the P.R.O. of a motor manufacturing company and you are asked to arrange facilities for a B.B.C. film unit to film in the works for a T.V. programme dealing with the motor industry. The film unit expect to be in the works for a period of ten days.

Outline what you would do to organize facilities for the film unit.

List any suggestions you would put to the film director to secure presentation of your Chairman in the film.

State your views on the possibilities of local press publicity for this happening and what you would do to arrange it.

5. You are the P.R.O. promoting a new, attractively packed, modestly priced and nationally distributed perfume.

You are required to send black and white photographs of this product and pack to the National and Sunday press, and the provincial daily and Sunday press.

State: (i) What qualities you would look for in the photographs?

(ii) How would you caption these photographs?

(iii) In what form would you post them?

(iv) Add any comment on timing that you think relevant.

6. You are the Press Officer for an exhibition which is related to British exports. The exhibition has been open two days out of a total of ten days. A leading correspondent of an American newspaper, such as *The New York Times* or *The Wall Street Journal*, calls at the Press Office and says: 'I need an exclusive photograph to back up my story. The President of your exhibition is coming down tomorrow morning to meet a leading American buyer. Can you arrange the picture for me and send it to my office?'

State what you would do in this case and give some indication of the timing of your action.

7. You are the P.R.O. of an industrial organization. Your company has been free from industrial disputes but the industry has experienced a lot of troubles from strikes. You are called upon to brief a photographer to photograph your Chairman presenting a gold watch on the factory floor to a shop steward who has completed 21 years' service with the firm.

Write the brief and indicate the press list for distribution of the picture.

8. A manufacturer of high class laboratory measuring equipment makes and distributes first class 16 mm., full-colour films as an audio-visual aid for teaching science in technical colleges. The films are distributed without cost to the users. The firm's literature is also distributed when the films are shown.

State your opinions of the value of this activity to the manufacturer.

9. Consider you are the P.R.O. of the Cunard Steam-ship Company and you have commissioned a set of 18 automatically projected 35 mm. coloured slides, and a set of top-class large-size black and white photographs, to illus-trate the principles of design of the interior of the 'Queen Elizabeth II'.

These visual aids are intended to be made available to art schools and colleges as a free aid to help in the teaching of 'Design'.

A headmaster writes to you and says: 'My students are second year, keen and industrious, which of these two sets do you recommend for me?'

Give your reasons for recommending the slides or photo-graphs.

10. Presume you are called upon to brief an artist to design three full colour wall charts for free distribution to Self-Service and Supermarket grocery outlets dealing with

the introduction of the Decimal Coinage on 15 February, 1971. The print order will be 100,000 copies of each poster. Write your brief to the artist.

11. You are the P.R.O. of a manufacturer of a well-established, good quality cake mixture. In connection with a two-year education–public relations campaign you have to make a decision to use:

Either (a) Well produced literature with a generous sample of the product distributed free three times a year to domestic science teachers;

or (b) Demonstrations at food exhibitions throughout the country, where you can sample products made by the cake mixture but you cannot sell the mixture.

Consider that both forms of activity cost the same and that you can have only one in your campaign for two years. State your case for either (a) or (b).

12. You are asked by a leading hair stylist to produce a series of colour slides to be shown in his hair styling salons for ladies.

The slides are to show hair styling and hair colouring techniques. The complete set is 12 slides and he plans to use at least thirty sets in automatic projectors, and to carry on the idea for two years.

List, with a brief description of each slide, what you would recommend for this series.

Also state how you would deal with the problem of 'fashion' in hair styling and hair colouring over a period of two years.

# Associate Examination—15 and 16 December 1969

## Paper I—Three Hours

*Principles and Practice of Public Relations*

*Candidates are reminded that particular emphasis is placed on command of English. Candidates* **must** *attempt questions 1 and 2, and may answer any three others.*

1. You have been asked to give a lecture on public relations practice. List the points you would make in explaining the Institute's definition and give two other definitions which you consider would help your audience to grasp the significance of the practice.

2. The Institute of Public Relations is currently reviewing its Code of Professional Conduct. Discuss the value of the Code and why it should be retained in its present form; or, alternatively, outline your suggestions for its improvement.

3. The success of public relations practice lies in the accurate identification of the 'publics' of an organization or institution, and in directing communications systematically. Indicate typical publics of:
   (i) a local authority
   (ii) a toy manufacturer
   (iii) a departmental store
and, in the case of one of the above, indicate the principal media through which its publics might be reached.

4. Outline the structure and describe the set-up of any public relations department, section, or branch with which you may be familiar, explain its method of budgetary control, and indicate its place in the organization's administration as a whole. If you consider the arrangements described produce the best results, explain why. On the other hand, if

you believe they could be made more effective, discuss the steps you would advise to secure an improvement.

5. Draft a check list of the main methods of assessing the results of public relations activities, and describe two in detail.

6. What are the functions of a public relations consultancy? Describe the Institute of Public Relations' recommendations on fees and methods of charging for public relations services.

7. 'The spoken word is the oldest means of communication and it still remains a very powerful medium of public relations.'
Discuss this statement, and indicate the steps you would advise to ensure that spokesmen for your organization are adequately equipped to put up a performance likely to enhance its reputation or 'image'.

8. What is meant by the term 'community relations'?
Describe some typical methods adopted by industrial concerns to secure good community relations, if possible quoting specific case-histories to illustrate your answer.

### Associate Examination—15 and 16 December 1969

#### Paper II—Three Hours

*Press Relations*

*Candidates* **must attempt questions 1 and 2** *and* **any three** *others*

(The term 'Press' includes sound radio, T.V. and newsreel films, etc. throughout the whole of this paper.)

*Press Relations II*

1. You have been appointed P.R.O. for an old established family manufacturing concern which has recently gone 'public'. Your chairman is worried about your company's financial image despite a satisfactory trading position. He thinks Press publicity would help remedy this. What Press programme would you put up to him?

2. Your directors are meeting tomorrow to finalize an announcement of major importance to the company's employers and shareholders. You have just received a call from a *Financial Times* reporter who has two-thirds of the story and informs you that it is proposed to use his story in the next day's issue. What would you do?

3. A major British company with world wide ramifications is revealing to the Press a revolutionary plant for high speed tyre testing. To obtain maximum international public exposure of this exciting machinery it is essential that the bulk of the Press coverage should be visual. What arrangements would you make to ensure the achievement of this objective? You have two Press officers to assist you and you may assume a budget of £5,000.

4. As Press officer you are asked by your employer to help launch a new range of household vinyl floor covering. It is

suggested that a Press conference be held to launch this exciting 'new look' in floor coverings. What would your recommendations be for the timing of the Press launch, how the flooring should be shown, and, broadly, what Press should be involved? You have one assistant and a budget of £1,500.

5. The directors of a major company have decided to remove one of their colleagues from the board. The circumstances are such that both parties have agreed to the exact wording of an announcement which the company feels must be made in its shareholders' interests. Minimum publicity, however, is required. How would you set about this? You have 48 hours in which to act.

6. An appliance manufacturer is planning to introduce to the U.K. market a new electric frying pan, with thermostatic control for the correct cooking of different dishes. A major Press campaign is required but your budget is only £1,000. How would you achieve the necessary impact in all media—Press, radio, television, newsreels—and how would you make this last?

7. The Army has decided to establish a small arms training school near a local well-frequented beauty spot. You have been engaged by local residents to start a protest campaign against this proposal by the Ministry of Defence, which would strictly limit access to the beauty spot. The noise from the school would also be detrimental to wild life in the area. Maximum sympathetic support is required from the national and local Press to overturn this decision—what recommendations would you make?

8. A Local Authority, long noted for its archaic ways in dealing with the Press, have surprisingly appointed a town manager. One of his first discoveries was the alarming apathy shown to the authority by the local populace and Press. As

an outside consultant you are called in to advise on how to
remedy this situation, particularly through the Press, as this
is considered the quickest, most effective and least expensive
way. What recommendations for a course of action would
you place before the town manager ?

# Associate Examination—15 and 16 December 1969

## Paper III—Three Hours

*Printed material, house journals, advertising*

Candidates must answer **Four** questions: **question 1** *and* **one question** *from each of Sections A, B and C.*

*Questions 1 carries 40 marks; the other three questions carry 20 marks each.*

### 1. (**Compulsory**)

The Managing Director of a large group of insurance companies has decided to devote a major part of his talk to shareholders, at the Company's Annual General Meeting, to the topic of: 'The increasing importance of our Advertising, Printed Material and House Journals'. This talk will subsequently be reproduced in the Company's printed Annual Report.

The Company publishes two house journals, for policy-holders and for staff respectively, and operates a profit-sharing scheme through which employees can hold shares in the group. In addition to its own advertising, the Company contributes to a co-operative advertising campaign mounted by the insurance industry.

The Managing Director has asked you, the P.R.O. of the group, to prepare an outline brief on which he could base his talk. He has specifically requested that you view the three promotional activities mentioned in the light of their effect on consumer demand, on staff relationships, and on the economy of the country at large.

Prepare a memorandum setting out the cardinal points you feel he should cover in his talk, commenting briefly on the reason for their importance.

*Section A      Printed Material      Answer* **one** *question only*

2. Your organization is to produce a new booklet. State, giving reasons, what factors would influence your choice of printing process.

3. (*a*) Explain, with the aid of diagrams, the differences in printing surface used in the major printing processes.

   (*b*) Describe briefly the characteristics of each method.

   (*c*) Indicate the type of work for which each method is best suited.

*Section B      House Journals      Answer* **one** *question only*

4. You have been asked to address your fellow students on a week-end course, on the subject of 'What the P.R.O. should know about House Journals'. Outline the points you would make in a 20 minute talk.

5. Name and describe any House Journal which you consider to be effective, giving reasons for your choice and commenting on its editorial policy and format, its circulation, and on the specific objectives you consider this particular House Journal is intended to achieve.

*Section C      Advertising      Answer* **one** *question only*

6. List and comment on the major steps to be taken in planning and executing an advertising campaign.

7. Write brief notes on FIVE of the following:

Advertising Appropriation    The agency commission system
Readership    A.B.C.
Copy Platform    Storyboard
Plans Board    Direct Mail
Evaluation of results    Media Scheduling

## Associate Examination—15 and 16 December 1969

### Paper IV—Three Hours

**Please** *read the questions carefully*

*Candidates are required to answer* **question one,** *either* **question two** *or* **three** *and* **any** *three other questions.*

**All** *questions carry the same marks*

1. What are the public relations activities you would consider organizing in support of a stand at a trade fair in the United Kingdom and what extra activities might be appropriate if the trade fair is being held overseas?

(Complete your answer in not more than 300 words.)

2. Prepare a draft budget for a stand at Olympia at the Mechanical Handling or similar exhibition. Assume that your company makes large items of equipment and that your stand will be 1,000 square feet. The actual figures of costs can be approximate but make sure you include all the likely costs.

3. If you were organizing a conference or a series of lectures, what are the different types of visual aids which you might be asked to provide for individual lecturers? Give some comments on the relative merits of these different types of visual aids.

4. Discuss the advantages and disadvantages of a company's public relations department making its own films or using the services of a professional film making company.

5. How would you organize the photographic section of your public relations department? List the staff you would need and the likely costs. Discuss whether it is a good thing to have your own photographic section or not.

6. How has the wide spread of television affected the use and value of public relations films?

7. Discuss the use of photographs (1) in house journals; (2) in connection with exhibitions; and (3) with press releases; and mention any differences of approach that are desirable for these different fields.

8. What differences are there between trade fairs and exhibitions? What is your opinion of the value of world fairs such as Expo '70 in Osaka?

### Membership Examination—17 April 1969

### Paper I—Three Hours

*Background Subjects*

*Candidates are required to answer four questions—both questions in Section 1; one question in Section 2; and one question in Section 3.*

### Section 1—Answer **both** questions

1. How would you define 'management'? What are the main resources, responsibilities and objectives of the top management of a privately-owned industrial firm?

2. One of the features of the twentieth century has been the development of what is now known as 'public relations' and its increasing recognition as a specialized activity. What are the fundamental reasons for this development?

### Section 2—Answer **one** question only

3. Give your views on both of the following:
(*a*) whether the growth of tribunals operating outside the traditional courts of law is desirable or otherwise, and whether it should be further encouraged or not.
(*b*) the 'pros and cons' of the division of the legal profession into two main branches—barristers and solicitors.

4. If you sue a newspaper for libel, what must you prove for your action to succeed? What defences are available to the newspaper? And how, if at all, can you defeat those defences?

### Section 3—Answer **one** question only

5. Describe some of the main recommendations of (*a*) the Maud Report on Management in Local Government; and (*b*) the Fulton Report on the re-organization of the Civil Service.

6. Outline briefly some of the proposals that have lately been put forward for change in the British system of industrial relations. (These include the Donovan Report, the Government's White Paper 'In Place of Strife', and policy documents from the Opposition parties.) Give your personal views as to the practicability of whatever proposals you mention.

## Membership Examination—17 April 1969

### Paper II—Three Hours

*Public Relations in Practice*

**Four questions** *to be answered. Nos.* **one** *and* **two** *are compulsory. The remaining two may be chosen from Nos.* **three, four, five** *or* **six.** *Provided answers are clearly numbered the questions may be answered in any order.*

1. A businessman, faced with intense competition from a rival company which is constantly in the news and whose chairman has become a T.V. celebrity, invites P.R. consultancies to present proposals for P.R. on his behalf. The annual fee offered is £7,000 plus expenses. He is perfectly frank about wanting to outdo his successful rival, and says that the contract will be awarded to the consultancy which can promise him the best results.

As a member of the Institute bound to uphold the principles of the Code of Professional Conduct, what is your reaction to this agreement, bearing in mind your eagerness to acquire new business? Would you have any objections to his proviso, or could you reconcile yourself to this challenge which he regards as a thoroughly reasonable and businesslike demand? In answering the above questions assume that you are submitting detailed proposals on a professional basis and *write the section in which you specifically deal with this aspect of the assignment.*

2. If you were considering the use of an opinion survey what would determine your choice of either a random or a quota sample?

*Answer two only from the following four questions*

3. A famous private company with headquarters outside London is to launch its first public share issue in three

P

months' time. Four million five shilling ordinary shares will be offered at twenty-five shillings each in order to finance expansion, including the development of the firm's export trade. No specialist financial P.R. consultant is either employed or contemplated. As the company's staff P.R.O. what techniques would you recommend to your Board to exploit fully the P.R. potential of this important step in the history of your company?

4. You have been shortlisted for the position of P.R. consultant to a local authority which is anxious to attract both industry and residents but is not prepared to set up its own P.R. department. There is a public relations committee which has done little more than discuss whether the Council should employ a P.R.O. or appoint a consultant. No one on the committee has any commercial experience of P.R., and some are frankly sceptical about spending the ratepayers' money in this way. How would you answer the committee chairman's question: 'In the light of the criticisms of P.R. you have heard from the Committee, in what ways do you feel you can help us?'

5. You are P.R.O. of a voluntary body which carries out an important, well-known and respected service. It is commonly believed, however, that it is a service financed from public funds. Prepare a six-months' programme of P.R. activities aimed at demonstrating to possible donors that the body is not financed out of public funds but is utterly dependent upon voluntary donations. For obvious reasons, your budget is negligible!

6. The Ministry of Transport is determined to improve road safety on motorways during bad weather. As chief information officer you have been instructed to prepare a draft scheme of P.R. activities for the Minister's approval. This can include a budget for poster and T.V. advertising if necessary.

There is considerable data available on accidents, road surface experiments and installation of warning lights, etc. But, as an essential part of this P.R. operation you believe that the first step is to find out more about *why* the accidents occur. Consider what research techniques (other than opinion research) you could employ for this purpose, and how you would apply your findings in a P.R. programme. *Then prepare an outline of your eventual report on these two-part proposals, showing how they depend on two-way communication.*

## Membership Examination—18 April 1969

### Paper III—Three Hours
*Case History*

*Candidates are required to answer **one**, and only one, of the following questions. You are free, if you wish, to quote actual cases, and your answers will be treated in the strictest confidence.*

1. *The Problem*

You are the Public Relations chief of Air Britain, an international airline which has provisionally ordered six supersonic airliners from British manufacturers who have just begun flight tests with the aircraft. The Board of the airline has requested you to submit a plan to deal in particular with the following formidable P.R. problems:

(i) The provisional order stipulated among other conditions that Air Britain would not confirm it unless on completion of the tests (a) the aircraft, capable of accommodating 120 passengers and flying at 1,350 m.p.h., would be an economic proposition when an average of 80 persons were carried on each journey between the U.K. and the U.S.A., the route on which the aeroplane is due to operate regular services; and (b) the noise of the aircraft was within the limits laid down by the British and American authorities.

As there has been criticism in Parliament and the Press that in imposing conditions (a) and (b) above the airline has shown a lack of faith in the competence of a world famous British manufacturer, there is a need for Air Britain to explain convincingly to the public the reasons for these conditions.

(ii) On the assumption that in due course the aircraft will get its Certificate of Airworthiness and that it is otherwise fully acceptable to the airline, Air Britain anticipates that at least initially there will be reluctance among a considerable number of air travellers to fly in such a revolutionary type of airliner. It will thus be necessary to mount a campaign to remove these doubts.

(iii) A widespread campaign is being developed in the U.K. by an 'anti-supersonic aircraft' group, with the support of influential people, on the grounds that the noise of the aeroplane will cause severe and unwarranted disturbance to the peace of millions of U.K. inhabitants living below the land route of the airliner. Air Britain believes that in co-operation with the manufacturers it must take urgent steps to counteract the fears of the public, especially as the aircraft will not fly at a supersonic speed until it is over the Atlantic and as sonic booms will not occur over land.

## The Question

Outline the 1969 P.R. plan for the U.K. that you would propose for the approval of your Board. What media would you intend to use—and why? Out of a total of £1¼ million available for the whole campaign £1 million has been allocated to advertising, leaving £¼ million for the implementation of your P.R. plan.

## 2. The Problem

You are a senior account executive of a British P.R. consultancy which has been commissioned to organize in the western world a fund-raising and publicity campaign for a newly-formed charitable Trust that aims to establish medical clinics and flying doctor services in three carefully selected developing countries in Africa. At present facilities of this kind are either unavailable or are very limited in scope. You have been assigned to the job of organizing the campaign.

It is appreciated by the organizers of the Trust that even many millions of pounds would be inadequate to deal effectively with the problem but they calculate that a useful start could be made if initially £2½ million were raised. They have told the consultancy that they consider the immediate P.R. task is (a) to make the objects of the Trust known to the public as widely as possible; and (b) to formulate plans to raise money for the proposed work to be done in the three countries.

If the campaign is to be successful it is essential to gain widespread public sympathy for the cause and also the confidence of the western world public in the ability of the Trust to fulfil its mission, which already has the warm support of internationally eminent people.

The proposed locations of the clinics and flying doctor service bases have been agreed with the Governments of the three countries, providing adequate funds are obtained, but so far little has been made known of the reasons that have led the Trust to undertake the work. You are therefore required to make a thorough survey of the whole project and of the opportunities it can offer to bring medical aid to the scattered inhabitants of the countries concerned.

## The Question

What recommendations would you make to the Trust for carrying out the foregoing requirements and what is your estimate of the approximate time it will take to produce your proposals to launch the campaign? You can assume that the Trust, if satisfied with your plans, will be prepared to meet the cost provided it is within reasonable limits.

## 3. *The Problem*

A large confectionery firm, which has lately merged with a smaller company making the same kind of products, has decided that the P.R. activities of the newly combined undertaking are highly important. Hitherto the larger firm has relied on the services of a Press Officer and two assistants and the smaller concern has depended on its sales department to deal with its Press publicity.

The new undertaking, faced with strong competition at home and in its overseas markets, which are primarily in the major Commonwealth countries, has accordingly appointed you as its chief P.R.O., responsible to the Chairman and Executive Management. You are not in charge of advertising but top management expects you to obtain as extensive Press editorial, sound radio, T.V. and film publicity as possible for its products.

The Chairman and most members of the Executive Managements realize that it is not easy to get Press publicity for particular brands of confectionery but a stubborn and vigorous Sales Director believes that because the firm has a fine reputation newspapers will be ready to give it editorial mention for that reason alone. You thus have an internal problem which can well create difficulties for you.

Both companies involved in the merger have efficient and up-to-date factories and from time to time have introduced new methods and machines but whereas the staff relations of the larger of the firms have been good, those of the smaller one have often been unsatisfactory. Moreover, the larger one has built an attractive housing estate for its workers and has organized social and recreational clubs for them. The smaller firm has not.

### *The Question*

Explain in some detail how you would organize your P.R. set-up so that in your opinion you would be able to do the work required of you, on the assumption that the company is prepared to meet the cost, provided you do not seek a greatly increased staff or too lavish a department. What new appointments would you wish to make and how would you plan an effort, not only to get increased Press and similar publicity, but to improve the general P.R. of the firm, bearing in mind the problems mentioned? Indicate clearly how, in your view, you could obtain the publicity which your employers want.

## Communication Advertising and Marketing Education Foundation

## Public Relations Certificate Scheme

### Stage 1—Paper 2

## SYLLABUS FOR BUSINESS ORGANIZATION

*Aim*

The purpose of this syllabus is to give a broad survey of business organization, the functions of key departments, and business environments.

Marketing is omitted as this is dealt with as a separate subject.

1. *Business Units*

    Sole trader, partnerships, public and private companies, co-partnerships, co-operative undertakings, nationalized industries.
    The role of professional institutions, trade associations, and the trade unions.
    Interlocking and holding companies; amalgamations and mergers.

2. *Finance*

    Balance sheets and profit and loss accounts.
    Budgets and financial control; break-even analysis; relations with marketing and production functions.
    Banking and insurance; company financial structure: stocks and shares, financial gearing.

3. *Organization*

    Formal and work-flow structures and relationships.
    Co-ordination, co-operation and delegation.
    Communications.

4. *Production*
    Types of production (job, batch, mass, flow).
    Deployment of resources (materials, labour, machines).
    Elements of work study.

    Purchasing and stock control; relations with marketing and finance function.
    Research and development.

5. *Personnel*
    Job analysis.
    Recruitment, training, motivation, development and assessment of individuals.
    Distinctive roles of management and supervision.
    Group factors.

6. *Environment*
    Relations between the firm and organized groups outside it—suppliers, customers, financial backers, trade unions.
    Central and local government social and economic policy; central and local government controls; the increasing participation of government in business activity.
    Maintenance of corporate identity versus individual company personality. Monopolies and cartels.

## Communication Advertising and Marketing Education Foundation

## Public Relations Certificate Scheme

## Stage 2—Paper 6

# SYLLABUS FOR HUMAN RELATIONS IN INDUSTRY AND COMMERCE

*Aim*

The aim of this syllabus is to provide the candidate with an understanding of the human aspects involved in day to day business operations and of the Public Relations Officer's relationship with Personnel and Training Officers, Line and Top Management.

The relationship with the Business Organization syllabus should be noted.

1. *Organization at work*

Organizations as devices for distributing tasks and co-ordinating activities for the achievement of corporate goals: organizations as social systems: organizations as socio-technical systems.

Some major current management theories: relevance of research in the social and behavioural sciences: 'opinion leaders' at work and in the community.

Influences of technology on organizations: computer-ization: automation: influences of productivity agree-ments: management information systems, suggestions schemes.

2. *Employee relations*

Transition from school to work: education and training:

apprenticeships: craft skills and autonomy: industrial training boards.

Work and non-work: factors in work involvement and work alienation: the predicament of foremen.

Re-location of works: effects on wives and families: effects on work attitudes: effects on community being left and on community being entered.

### 3. *Industrial relations*

Conflict and conciliation.

Consultation, participation, joint consultative committees, joint councils.

Productivity Agreements.

The need to avoid misunderstandings by means of good and continuous communication.

The strategies of independence: professional groups: shop stewards and the groupings they represent: trade unions.

Trade Unions: history of movement, reforms to date, Donovan Report, 'In place of strife', the mid-1969 watershed, relationship of trade unions with central government.

### 4. *Employee loyalties*

Characteristics of workers in different occupational roles (assembly line, white collar, professional).

Influence of occupation on family life, leisure, social and political attitudes.

Relationships between economic class, cultural class and aspirations.

Stature of company in the community and the effect on employees.

Value of good communications in periods of stress— strike in progress, rumoured take-over, rumoured merger, rumoured shut down, rumoured redundancies.

5. *Personnel and P.R. functions*

Internal surveys of attitudes among employees, assistance the P.R.O. can give to Personnel.

Safety and good housekeeping: corporate safety policy: the P.R.O. as specialist aide to Personnel and Training Officers.

Importance of local press relations with regard to recruitment and turnover of personnel.

Purposes and values of works wall sheets: staff newspapers: house journals: communications of credibility versus management handouts.

The Personnel function: the Public Relations function: areas of overlapping interests and mutual assistance.

## Communication Advertising and Marketing Education Foundation

### Public Relations Certificate Scheme

### Stage 1—Paper 1

## SYLLABUS FOR PUBLIC RELATIONS

*Aim*

This syllabus provides the candidate with a knowledge of the professional context in which people working full time in public relations must carry out their day to day tasks and discharge their responsibilities.

1. *P.R. as a management function*

   History of public relations.
   Definition: concept: principles.
   The service nature of public relations: the P.R.O. as a channel of two-way information and communication.
   Desirable personal characteristics and temperamental traits: the question of personal integrity.

2. *The Institute of Public Relations*

   History. I.P.R. Committees and their functions. Services to members. Members' responsibilities to Institute. Institute's relationships with international and other national public relations bodies and institutions.

3. *Ethics of public relations*

   The Institute's Code of Professional Practice. Reasons behind each Clause. Protection afforded to members.

4. *Laws affecting public relations practice*

   N.B. An introductory talk on the English and Scottish legal systems and the system of the Courts is recommended.
   Company law: what it is; the essence of Contract:

Defamation: Copyright: Trade Descriptions Act 1968: Merchandise Marks Act(s): Consumer Protection: Trade Marks, Patents: Restrictive Practices: Monopolies: Children and Young Persons Act 1969 (in relation to young 'performers' for still or moving photography).

5. *Psychology of communication*

Theory. Language, perception, reception, meaning.
The art of communicating. McLuhan's concept.
Comparative studies of impact of speech, the written word, visual presentations.
The contribution of technology to the modern communications 'explosion': the shrinking world.

Public relations, persuasion, propaganda.

6. *P.R. practice in organizational frameworks*

Staff: Consultancies: Central government press and information officers: Local government public relations.
Counselling: counselling/services: services only: personal and product publicity.
*Operational P.R.:* problem analysis: programme planning: costing and budgetary control: case presentation to client or management: programme execution: assessment of results.

## Communication Advertising and Marketing Education Foundation

## Public Relations Certificate Scheme

### Stage 2—Paper 4

## SYLLABUS FOR MEDIA—P.R. SERVICED

*Aim*

This syllabus is intended to be an intensive, high level course covering broad concepts, not detailed items. Its purpose is to provide candidates with an understanding of those media which are under editorial control and which P.R.O's serve by providing information or facilities or both.

N.B. This paper should be taken together with Paper 5, 'Media—P.R. Directed'.

1. *Print*

    Structure of the newspaper industry.
    The magazine, trade, technical and professional journal fields.

2. *Radio and television*

    Structure: coverage.
    State corporations: commercial companies.

3. *Internal organization of above media*

    Departmental breakdowns.
    Who does what: comparative responsibilities.

4. *Professional attitudes*

    Editorial approach.
    Professional attitudes of the journalist in each medium.

5. *Timing and handling of material*

    What is 'News'.
    When material is handled: how material is treated.

Essential information on mechanical processes in each
medium.

6. *Libel, slander, intrusion, copyright* (see also Section 4,
Paper 3)
Case histories: the rights of editors to publish in the
public interest: protection of sources of information:
the Press Council: the I.T.A.

7. *Central Office of Information*
Activities: services provided: who does what in which
section.

Q

## Communication Advertising and Marketing Education Foundation

## Public Relations Certificate Scheme

## Stage 2—Paper 5

# SYLLABUS FOR MEDIA—P.R. DIRECTED

*Aim*

To ensure that the candidate will have thorough working knowledge of all means of communication and presentation over which the P.R.O. can exercise control.

N.B. This paper should be taken together with Paper 4, 'Media—P.R. Serviced'.

1. *Basic media*

| | |
|---|---|
| *Printed word/pictures* | advertising |
| | direct mail |
| | print material |
| | mechanical processes |
| | news releases |
| *Photography* | still |
| | films |
| | film strips |
| | film slides |
| | closed circuit television |
| *Charts, Plans, and Diagrams* | blackboards |
| | pinboards |
| | magnetic boards |
| | flannel graphs |
| | static or animated |
| *Audio/Tape media* | V.T.R. and E.V.R. |
| | tape recorder |

disc (wire)
closed circuit television

*Models and Displays*
*Public Speaking*          Live audiences
                           Filmed material
                           T.V. appearances
*Business gifts*

2. *Complex media*

   (i)   Royal and V.I.P. visits, special events, facility visits, social functions including protocol and customs.

   (ii)  Trade fairs, British Weeks and other in-store promotions, agricultural shows, exhibitions, mobile exhibitions and displays.

   (iii) Press conferences, conferences, seminars, symposia, business games (training/learning), business drama (selling), sales presentations.

   (iv)  Sponsored sporting and artistic activities.

   (v)   Sponsored educational programmes.

   (vi)  News releases, house journals, staff and distributors' newspapers, works wall sheets, annual reports and other stockholder communications.

   (vii) Foreign language material: translations and translating services.

3. *Detailed study of each medium or group of media*

   Description, characteristics, advantages, disadvantages. Costs — capital and running — major 'publics'/ audiences.

4. *Planning*

   (*a*) Objectives, relationship to total P.R., P.R. support operations, Corporate Identity.

(b) Design brief, aesthetics, copyright, performing
rights.
Buying contractual requirements.
Budget and budget control.
Project control, network analysis, critical path tech-
nique, methods of charting/plotting.

5. *Support Publicity*

Before . . . during . . . follow-up.
Piggybacking.

6. *Evaluation*

Research before, during and after: records of use and
'publics' exposed to.
Costing and cost-effectiveness. Comparative evaluations
of different means of communication.
Press clippings: guard books: maintenance.

## Communication Advertising and Marketing Education Foundation

## Public Relations Certificate Scheme

### Stage 1—Paper 3

SYLLABUS FOR MARKETING

*Aim*

This introductory course aims to provide students with a general understanding of the marketing concept, the function of marketing within the modern industrialized society, and the role of marketing in relation to business organization and management.

The course also examines the organization and management of the marketing function within the company; the main areas of marketing decision and the disciplines by which they are reached; and the various processes by which marketing policy is implemented and controlled and results evaluated.

1. *The Marketing Concept*

   An Introduction to Marketing:

   What is marketing? The origins and development of the 'marketing concept'. Its implications in terms of company philosophy, policy, organization. The importance of behavioural studies. The problems with which marketing is concerned. The relationship between marketing and the other main business functions: product research and development. Production, finance, personnel. The 'marketing-mix' approach. The factors influencing the mix.

2. *Organization and Control*

   How the marketing function is organized within the company. The production-orientated company. The marketing-orientated company. The role of the Brand Manager. Relations with other primary functions. Marketing's contribution to overall company policy.

The use of outside services: The specialist services and consultancies available—marketing, market research, auxiliary sales force, design services, advertising services, 'below the line' services. How work may be divided between company and outside services.

3. *The Mass Marketing Environment*

(*a*) Distribution:

The evolution of the channels of distribution—a brief history. The origins, functions and development of the various channels and methods.

Modern distribution patterns—The development of the modern complex patterns. Direct selling, independent outlets, multiples, co-operatives, department stores, voluntary chains and groups, concessions and shops within shops, privilege cards, selling by agents. Mail order. Credit trading. Cash and carry. Discount houses, etc. Today's main trends. The changing pattern. Increasing emphasis on supermarket and self-service. Implications for the future. Repeal of RPM.

Distribution Policy—and the factors (e.g. relationship between type of product and method of distribution) which influence it.

(*b*) The Consumer:

Socio-economic change since 1900. The way attitudes have changed. The gradual evolution up to 1939. The strengthening of the marketing attitude. The shift of the balance of power in the market place. The impact of the 1939–45 War. The immediate post-war years. The crucial 50's and 60's. The years of rapid change. The growing need for a scientific approach in studying these changes, in predicting trends, in measuring consumer behaviour.

4. *Industrial Marketing*

Its special characteristics and problems. Basic marketing principles for the selling of industrial products and services. Modern industrial marketing techniques. The industrial marketing mix. The use of research.

5. *International Marketing*

The many cultural, trading, distribution, psychological, political and consumer attitude differences. The variations in buying habits, media availability, advertising practices. The need for exact local knowledge. Sources of information. Sources of local research. Transportation problems. The vital need for local experience. Methods of operating in foreign markets.

6. *The Marketing Plan*

Market Research: Its aims, scope and methods. What we need to find out about product, market, distribution, consumer behaviour. The limitations of research. Its control and programming.

Market Research Techniques: Introduction to the basic sources of marketing data. Desk research. Field research. Methods. The questionnaire.

Planning Marketing Strategy: The main areas of marketing decision: Branding, Pricing, Packaging. Distribution, selling, merchandising, sales promotion, advertising, public relations.

Product Policy: What is a product? Deciding which products should be marketed. Branding, Pricing, Packaging. Development and testing. Deciding on policy for distribution, sales, advertising and promotion. Establishing Marketing Objectives, Marketing Budgets. Handling the marketing mix. Launching and maintaining a product.

Case histories for mass, industrial and international marketing.

7. *Sales Organization*

How the sales function is organized, administered, controlled. Sales training. Sales policy. Sales conferences. The use of auxiliary sales forces and merchandising forces. International sales management. Selection of local selling agents and problems of communication.

8. *The role of Advertising, Sales Promotion and Public Relations*

Establishing advertising and promotion objectives: The role of the company marketing/advertising departments. The role of the advertising agency. Relations and contact with the agency. Factors involved in planning and executing an advertising campaign. The purposes of promotions. The planning and control of promotional activity. The role of merchandising, public relations and corporate publicity.

9. *Controlling the Market Effort*

Evaluating and controlling marketing operations: The need to analyse and quantify the elements of the marketing mix in action. The detection of problem areas with regard to sales, advertising and promotion, distribution, competitive activity, budget, product development and consumer attitudes.

Test marketing: Aims and objectives, methods and control. Planning and executing, measuring results. Determining action to be taken.

# CONCLUSION

Leonard L. Knott, one of North America's best-known Public Relations consultants, has been in the profession for more than a quarter of a century. A past President of the Canadian Public Relations Society, he wrote a splendid book entitled *Plain Talk about Public Relations*, published by McClelland and Stewart, Ltd. Designed as a Public Relations primer for executives it deals with the businessman's dilemma when considering Public Relations:

'Is there any wonder businessmen are confused? If every truck driver, office clerk and telephone girl turns out to be a Public Relations representative, then what is all this twaddle about professional training, university degrees, and understanding and imaginative minds?' But business cannot win its battle for public acceptance alone.

'What is to be done?

'First, business executives must recognize that the problem exists, that it is their problem and that they alone must attempt to solve it. They must then with determination seek to remove from their own houses the evils, the foolishness and capriciousness which are known to exist. Together with other businessmen, including their competitors, they must determine to impose high standards of morality upon the entire business community. This requires a voluntary acceptance of an enforceable code of ethics similar to those supported by the professions.

'In the interests of world peace as well as for the preservation of international business, management everywhere must learn more about, and develop a respect for, foreign customs and manners no matter how strange or ridiculous these may seem to be.

'Individually and collectively, business executives need to study the ways and means by which the new attitudes of responsible enterprise can be communicated to all sections of the public first at home and then to nations abroad. This task will require more than a cursory study. It will need the services of an immense, thoroughly and honestly trained corps of Public Relations people. The job of training these people will be long and arduous and even if started right away would show few results in less than a decade.

'Basically the question of changing the public attitude towards business, both at home and abroad, becomes one of changing the public attitude of business towards itself. Business, is not, in spite of what so many people like to call it, a game. It is a serious part of life. It should no longer be treated as something of little importance, left to the mercy of exploiters and demagogues. If serious attention is not directed to this salvation neither business nor society will long remain free.'